New & Selected Poems

Also by Ron Padgett

Bean Spasms (with Ted Berrigan), 1967
Great Balls of Fire, 1969
The Adventures of Mr. & Mrs. Jim and Ron (with Jim Dine), 1970
Antlers in the Treetops (with Tom Veitch), 1970
Oo La La (with Jim Dine), 1973
Toujours l'amour, 1976
Tulsa Kid, 1979
Triangles in the Afternoon, 1979
Among the Blacks, 1988
Light As Air (with Alex Katz), 1988
The Big Something, 1990
Blood Work: Selected Prose, 1993
Ted: A Personal Memoir of Ted Berrigan, 1993

Translations

The Poet Assassinated by Guillaume Apollinaire, 1968
Dialogues with Marcel Duchamp by Pierre Cabanne, 1971
Kodak by Blaise Cendrars, 1976
The Poems of A. O. Barnabooth by Valery Larbaud (with Bill Zavatsky), 1977
Complete Poems by Blaise Cendrars, 1992

RON

PADGETT

NEW  SELECTED

POEMS

DAVID R. GODINE, PUBLISHER
Boston

This book is for Patricia

First published in 1995 by
David R. Godine, Publisher, Inc.
Box 9103
Lincoln, Massachusetts 01773

Some of the poems in this collection were previously published in the volumes
Great Balls of Fire (Holt, Rinehart & Winston/Coffee House Press),
Toujours l'amour (SUN), *Triangles in the Afternoon* (SUN),
Tulsa Kid (Z Press), and *The Big Something* (The Figures).
Acknowledgment is also made to the following publications,
in which the uncollected poems first appeared:
*Arshile, The Cafe Review, Cream City Review, Gas, The Herman Review,
New American Writing, Paris/Atlantic, Scripsi, Teachers & Writers,
Triage, Sulfur,* and *What!*
"Sleep Alarm" appeared in the anthology *Broadway.*
"Alphonse Goes to the Pharmacy" was published in a limited edition artist's book
designed by Bertrand Dorny.

Library of Congress Cataloging-in-Publication Data

Padgett, Ron.
[Poems. Selections]
New & selected poems / Ron Padgett.
by Ron Padgett.—1st ed.
p.   cm.
ISBN: 1-56792-038-1
I. Title.
PS3566.A32N49   1995
811'.54--DC20   95-15239 CIP

First edition
Printed in the United States of America

Contents

New & Selected Poems

American Cowslip

Nothing is
the way you think it is
going to be.
Take this little flower
from me, and let it go
into the way you think of it.
And so it grows
and is the face
of Daisy the cow speaking,
she my young grandma
growing and wearing
a pink slip and who fell
from the sky that was
clear blue and pure
all over the place
you called home
as it moved out
from under you
in the slow
rotation of the sphere
you call a star,
a flower, a mind.

Early Triangles •.

Can you feel the swell—
or is there one?—
of something vast & wonderful
coming over America?
Or is that just the glow
of lights from Montpelier?
I stood out in the woods
and spoke to the trees with their leaves,
and they answered back. They said,
"Jerome, Jerome,
return to your village."
I did so, and began

to lick postage stamps.
Red ones and green ones, some
with pink and yellow,
delicate triangles in the afternoon.

Getting Along

We stride briskly down the country lane, bluejay squabble overhead in the last wisps of fog, and the night's breath of the woods still around us. That's a poetic way of saying that we are two old farts out for a morning constitutional, like the gray-haired but trim couple in nice sports clothes who are walking, smiling and tanned, on the covers of magazines devoted to "the issues of health and aging." Those people, however, also have huge retirement funds, and will never have to "worry." On the one hand, I am a bit nonplussed at finding myself on a magazine cover, and on the other hand I like to think that, like these model people, as I age I will enjoy good health. I will not only walk down country lanes, but right up the sides of houses and over their tops–to leave the doctor's office after my annual checkup, I will simply crash through the walls. I will approach the condition of the scientist who not only died and came back to life, but was able to rearrange the molecular structure of sticks and leaves to form a cowboy hat. I will walk unafraid through a forest of cowboy hats.

Talking to Vladimir Mayakovsky •*

All right, I admit it:
        It was just a dream I had last night.
                I was trudging along a muddy path
in a column of downcast men
        on the blackened outskirts of New York,
              the twilight dingy and ruined,
the future without hope
        as we marched along
             in our soiled, proletariat rags.
To my left was Mayakovsky, head shaved,
        and next to him his friend
             with gray beard and dark cap.

"You've got to admit," Mayakovsky
          was saying, "that this is a pretty good
                    way to write a poem."
"Yes, " I said, "the momentum
          is sustained by our walking forward,
                    the desolate landscape seeps into every word,
and you're free to say anything you want."
          "That's because we're inside the poem,"
                    he said, "not outside." Puddles
of oily water gleamed dully beneath the low clouds.
          "That's why my poems were so big:
                    there's more room *inside*."
The hard line of his jaw flexed and
          the men dispersed. I followed
                    his friend behind a wall
to hear the poem go on
          in the lecture the friend was giving on history,
                    but no, the real poem had finished.
I went back to the spot
          where the poem had finished.
                    Vladimir had left the poem.

Déjà Vu

I'm back in the saddle again,
splitting every situation into three equal parts
and hearing the voice of Aunt Jemima
emerge from the Delphic Oracle.
It's pancake time in Greece, huge
flapjacks draped over the countryside:
shadows of moving clouds,
blotches of ideas projected down
from the great old Mr. Everything,
he who at this very moment checks his watch
and looks down at me.

Haiku

First: five syllables
Second: seven syllables
Third: five syllables

♣

Air
Light
Energy
& Love
All so wonderful
To be a part of
& have them be
part you:
Light so sweet
& Air so mild
Energy so great
& Love so wild
& Crazy when
It hits you
Hard & All
At once & then
is gone
& you with it

But it comes back
You know
bigger & better
& harder than
ever before
This is true
& I
am here to
tell you so

Louisiana Perch •

Certain words disappear from a language:
their meanings become attenuated,
grow antique, insanely remote or small,
vanish.
          Or become something else:
transport. Mack
the truck driver falls for a waitress
    where the water flows. The

great words are those without meaning:
    from   a   their   or
    Or   the   for   a   the
    The   those

The rest are fragile, transitory
    like the waitress, a

beautiful slender young girl!
I love her! Want to
marry her! Have hamburgers!
Have hamburgers! Have hamburgers!

Autumn's Day

Rilke walks toward a dime. I saw.
It was very great. But now
His shadow is fast upon the sundials.
How then can the winds remind
The shadows it is late?

"Who has no home cannot build now,"
Said Rilke to a grasshopper.

Little grasshopper,
You must waken, read, write long letters, and
Wander restlessly when leaves are blown.

The Statue of a Libertine

I've chosen this title not only because I like it
But also it embodies the kind of miniature grandness
A toy instrument has, or powerful dwarf, half sinister
Half pleasure and unexplained

Now I address the statue

Lips that were once as volatile
As similes spoken by an insane person
Who resembled the carving of an irrational human being
But one endowed with such sweetness the pockets are
Blown to bits through their emptiness,

There is no margin of doubt to this reverse
Power, it moves back immediately, a Leonardo's square
You start back from—it extends a confusing,
Buffered metric scale of being
Toward the deep green velvet
That makes sleep possible
Near the gravel smitten with the gloam's evocative power—
these unintentionally horrible memories cling like peaches to the walls
Of the streets where stilettos whiz swiftly toward an incorrect mansion,
     probably

Not very pleasant thoughts
MOVE TOO QUICKLY

What's happening is that we're pawning especially
The vegetation
                    Watch it   There was a first light of print
Then suddenly my view of things
Either enlarges or contracts incredibly
And all I can see is the two of us, you
With your long dark hair, me looking at you hair against the screen
In this small kitchen with its yellow and white curtains
Shot into place with light
And everything else is gone forever
If it does nothing else, this feeling, at least
It relieves my temporal worries
And then it dawns on you: you're looking at the background

For every painting you've ever seen!
It's a kitchen exactly like this one
Containing the orange juice and two dozen eggs
And the coffee pot, the electric
One Tessie and I posed on either side of just before our trip to Rome
We went flying over Rome in a giant aspirin
We didn't see much but were free from headache
(This on a postcard home)
Moving up I thought I'd have the aspirin turn to powder
Which would fall on the city–the echo
I didn't answer because not answering is one of the luxuries
We have here, if we have a phone....
But enough of this, my head

The sun is now going up and down so fast I can hardly keep track of
what day today is–it's the next day, in fact, though it shouldn't be: I'm
wearing the same clothes, smoking the same cigarette, the temperature
is the cigarette. There is less darkness outside, though;

Unfortunately, I can't seem to fit it into any reasonable sequence–
                    one hundred fashionable yachts burning
Remind me of a Blaise Cendrars poem about yachts
I translated in Paris
A few minutes before seeing a young girl break
Down and cry in the Boulevard Saint-Germain. Thomas Hardy
Was with her but didn't seem to notice she was sobbing horribly and
I felt like pushing both of them into the traffic light
My bus had stopped at

     2.

Higher up, the wrist assumes a puffiness
Not unlike a pajama leg stuffed with hundred dollar bills
But a dramatic resolution is passed
Into the extended index finger whose rushing
Detonates the very tip

December •

I will sleep
in my little cup

Sweet Pea •

You are sweeter than the sweet pea
that climbs high and blooms
in early summer, mixed colors
pink, purple, blue, and red;
few flowers have the charm
you have, and few flowers
have the charm of the Sweet William,
but you have more charm
than the Sweet William, the Perfection
even. The Sunset Cosmos
flames in orange and scarlet:
you are more beautiful than the Sunset Cosmos.
The Mammoth Yellow Mum is more beautiful
than the Sunset Cosmos and you
are more beautiful than the mum,
you are more astounding than
super racy glads, assorted
colors, every color imaginable.
When I'm with you
terrific colors exist
unknown to the Super Gladiolus,
colors the Sonny Boy or Azure Blue,
the Climbing Crimson Glory or riotous Color Carnival
or the happy Swiss Giant Pansy
never attain, though they fly
upward through their hybrid generations
madly seeking the brilliance that is yours,
the brilliance morning glories strive
to equal in their matinal wide-awakeness,
the Pearly Gates opening to trumpet,
the Wedding Bells announcing, the Moonflower
glowing ethereal in its suave fragrance,

the Heavenly Blue—there is no flower
quite so blue as Heavenly Blue, its blue
reflected in the heavens
where light comes from, and when
I realize all the light
that goes to make a flower
I realize how much has gone
into making you whose presence is more
to me than all the heaven's blue.

For you are more spectacular than Champagne Bubbles
flown from Iceland, more amazing than the Presto
appearing at a magician's fingertips and more gracious
than the petunia, the Pinwheel spinning,
the Blue Mist drifting in bliss, Victory
flying high, Plum Purple heavy and sensual,
the wild throw-up-your-hands Elite Mixture,
the gorgeous foaming red ambiance of the Warrior, the
enormous blossoms of the Cream Whiz, the
funny snobbism of the Tiffany, more
sociable than phlox, Twinkle or Dwarf Star,
more absolutely engaging than the primrose
in its distant suggestiveness,
blooming in shade. The fantastic big blooms
of Oriental Poppies draw wild visions
from the brain, but you are wilder and
more visionary than the poppy, shooting
higher with brilliant trail, like the Rocket
Snap, the magnificent tall hybrids, or the
Bright Butterflies flying, crazy and excited,
the Madame Butterfly with its aplomb,
the sobs of the Little Duffer. You are more
beautiful than the Little Duffer. You are
more alert than the zinnia, more
mysterious than Lipstick, deeper than the
deep lavender of Dream Zinnias where Blue
Magic flies, greater than the Great Scot on
a background of pretty Rosy Morn, adjusting
its petals like vain Fluffy Ruffles, goofier
than Knockout Mums and more of a knockout than

Goofy, quicker than Blue Blazing Ageratum, more
majestic in gloom than the dark vibrating blue of Lamartine
Delphiniums, more persistent in memory than Woody Woodpecker
that blooms with a tremendous announcement, darker
and more passionately terrifying than the Giant Señorita,
warmer than Big Smile, more marvelous and
punctual than Marvel-of-Peru Four O'Clocks,
whiter than the White Gardenia that leans
over the piano, like Oscar singing to Love Song
whose light pink blends into the Glitters,
and for me you are even more dazzling than
the most exaggerated memory of a Junior Prom:
you are more than all of these, it is
as if I were to take five hundred
handfuls of every kind of flower,
fling them into the air and see
them bloom immediately there.

You are forever with me
as if my just being alive were enough
to surround me with the silver flames
of massive dahlias, cool and sexual
as Promise, the red blur of The
Cardinal perched on perfect stems
and then gone, the intriguing comic strip sexuality
of Kidd's Climax, the blasé bare shoulder
of New Look or Variety Girl, the moonlight
that shines down on D-Day. These are all
so beautiful! Blue Smoke over Albert
Schweitzer, Whirligig and Little Nemo, Visual
Illusion and Forever, Loves Me Loves Me Not,
Reynaldo Hahn and Equal Sign, Mahayana and
Angry Bumpkin, Out to Lunch, Magic Flute
and Dream Boat, Sunshine
and White Friendship, the quiescent
sentiment of Afterglow and
the yearning for the Infinite that is
in Bright Star—you are my Bright Star,
brighter than Superlative and fresher
than Baby's Breath, when it has just bloomed

and its pretty little flowers sigh
in delicate profusion, nodding gently in the air,
white in June and July. In June and July
is where I am when I'm with you,
the middle of the year, when looking back
and then ahead to the same amount of days,
means everything is in perfect balance,
you do not know if you are happy or sad,
who or where you are, you are
like the Senator Dirksen Marigold
now that the senator is dead–he has
become a flower.

You are not a flower, thank my lucky stars,
you are a woman, a girl, a moving
body of beauty, you are mine for nothing and
for no reason: the rain falls, the trees
stretch and yawn, the flowers fly
up out of the ground and burst
in zany gladness, constant as those lucky
stars I bless, bless for having you.

Beaujolais Villages

We have to wait. It's not yet time? But the door is still locked. The *patronne* has not yet arrived this morning. She was indisposed last night. That is, she was heaving her guts out down by the river, where she had staggered, alive and drunk under the weight of her anxiety over the shelling of her native city, far away, while here the people go on as if nothing were happening. Except, of course, they know that they do not understand why the cafe door remains shut and locked. The sunlight is hitting it at a slant, as if to say, Let me in, it is time to open up and let me in. The wooden door is growing ever brighter and warmer to the touch of the major as he shoves it first with his palms, then leans into it with his full body weight and makes it sag a bit. All those kilos converging with the sunlight on the door, and Arlette the pomeranian going by leaping and barking at little Michel who is holding a doggy treat just out of the reach of her snapping jaws.

Who and Each ·

I got up early Sunday morning
because it occurred to me that the word
which
might have come from a combination of *who* and *each*
and reached for the *OED*
which for me
(I think of it not
as the *Oxford English Dictionary*
but as the *O Erat Demonstrandum)*
has the last word:
"Hwelc, huelc, hwaelc, huaelc, huoelc, hwaelc, wheche, weche,
whech, qwech, queche, qheche, qwel, quelk, hwilc, wilc, hwilch,
wilch, whilc, whillc, whilk, whylke, whilke, whilk, wilke, whylk,
whilk, quilc, quilke, qwilk, quylk, quhylk, quilk, quhilk, hwic,
wic, hwich, wyche, wich, hwych, wiche, whiche, whyche, wych,
whych, which, quiche, quyche, quich, quych, qwiche, qwych,
qwyche, quhich, hwylc, hwulch, hulch, wulc, whulc, wulch,
whulche": Teutonic belching.
    But in little tiny type: "For the compounds *gewilc,
aeghwilc,* see *Each."*
Now, if you want to talk *belching*....
It was raining outside
with the blue-gray hiss of tires
against the wet street
I would soon walk my dog in,
the street I drove an airplane up
earlier this morning in a dream
in which the Latin word *quisque* appeared to me,
as if it meant *each which*
in the sea of *eisdem, quicumque,* and *uterque.*
Thus I spend my days,
waiting for my friends to die.

Yak and Yak ·

I am saying
that grammar is the direct result of how humans feel in the world;
or rather,
that grammar follows from what we experience viscerally and
punctuation keeps it that way;
that for instance, people walking down the street
are forming various sentences with their bodies,
and as the schoolgirl turns the corner the meaning
changes, oh so natural. Just so the wind
that suddenly turns the corner has just blown your hair off!
You go indoors and write,
"The wind has blown my hair away,"
then shift your weight and add, "almost."
For in your mind your arms have stretched to catch your head,
in which Pig Latin is understood but Dog not.
"Omecay erehay, etlay emay elltay ouyay omethingsay atthay
      ouyay ughtoay otay owknay."
In Hawaiian countries there was a battle over there,
anyhow, and when she heard the racket and the battle
of the fierce pineapples clashing under a warm moon,
she wrote across the sky, with her magic finger,
in glowing light, that she would not love her man anymore.
The palm trees stood like so many silent exclamation points
in the flowing beat of the night's heart.

More of This Light

This evening's clear light and light blue pink look like the Penguin
edition of *Elective Affinities,* but something was missing there, my
stomach is nervous, Goethe I should have said, and the deep green
of the fields was glowing an inwardly deeper green the blacktop
wound through and on which I sailed along, with just the first hint
of feeling that I might someday accept not being here anymore, if
only the light would stay this way.

To Woody Woodpecker ·

I love you, Woody,
when you peck
on the head
of a bad person
and laugh and fly
away real fast,
speed lines
in the air
and clouds of invisible
dust dissipating,
I love the way
you last only seven minutes.
The heart has seven minutes
with Woody Woodpecker,
seven minutes of pure bliss.

Hula

While I was writing my poem
Patty was doing the crossword puzzle
Hula was the word she got
Plus an all-expense paid trip to Hawaii

Now I live here all alone
A short fat figure made of grey stone
And as the flowers go past my door
I see their shadows move across the floor

The doughnut sings its pretty song
And so does sing the tellyvision
The purple martin flies for fun
The purple martin flies for fun

The purple martin flies for fun
Around the ego's solar system
Which hangs there like an illustration
That we are truly a great nation

Poem

Funny, I hear
Frank O'Hara's
voice tonight
in my head—
i.e. when I
think in words
he's saying them
or his tone
is in them.
I'm glad
I heard him
when he was alive
and I'm glad I can
hear him now
and not be sorry,
just have it all here,
the way Jimmy, stark
naked with rose petals
stuck to his body,
said, "Have you seen
Frank? I heard
he's in town tonight."

Wind

Now it is over and everyone knew it
The bad grass surrendered in unison and with much emotion
The long-awaited became despised
Everyone got tired and concluded that phase

Reports followed, causing intrusions
In the old-timers. Others go off for refreshment
The distrustful student prefers German popular songs
A language he does not understand

But now there is the tremendous reassurance of being
At the dinner table and tense, a stalwart melody

Tromping to its fluorescent conclusion.
This you find unimaginable, that rent should be suddenly so high
Up there in the cupola, the gauze
The tiny excitement of the generator
The note you read without even looking at it
Going back where you lose your hands you bask
Whitewash vistas a voice that finally remembers
Hedges that were once formidable
You watch and are horrified to be a part of it

The booth puts you out for miles this speedometer
The "fertile lowlands" you chalk it up in orange
And again a brush applies the proper lascivious colors
The postcard making it "right" instead of wrong

Nothing in That Drawer

Nothing in that drawer.
Nothing in that drawer.
Nothing in that drawer.
Nothing in that drawer.
Nothing in that drawer.
Nothing in that drawer.
Nothing in that drawer.
Nothing in that drawer.
Nothing in that drawer.
Nothing in that drawer.
Nothing in that drawer.
Nothing in that drawer.
Nothing in that drawer.
Nothing in that drawer.

Wonderful Things

Anne, who are dead   and whom I loved in a rather asinine fashion
                    I think of you often

        buveur de l'opium chaste et doux
                                    Yes I think of you
        with very little in mind

        as if I had become a helpless moron

                Watching zany chirping birds

            That inhabit the air

And often ride our radio waves

So I've been sleeping lately with no clothes on
The floor   which is very early   considering the floor
Is made of birds and they are flying and I am
Upsidedown and ain't it great to be great!!

Seriously I have this mental (smuh!) illness

                                which causes me to do things

                                        on and away
Straight for the edge
Of a manicured fingernail
Where it is deep and dark   and green   and silent

Where I may go at will
And sit down and tap

        My forehead against the sunset

Where he takes off the uniform
And we see he is God

God get out of here
And he runs off chirping and chuckling into his hand

And that is a wonderful thing

        …a tuba that is a meadowful of bluebells
is a wonderful thing

        and that's what I want to do

Tell you wonderful things

The Music Lesson

I would like to tell you a story.
My little wife suggested that I tell you this story
because she received such pleasure from it,
and I such pleasure in the telling.

Once there was a musical note.
It had a thin black stem, a black bulbous dot
on its side at the bottom, and on top a
single line jetting back. The note
lived in a universe whose time was equal
to its space: one could move through
this world by staying put and waiting
until enough time had passed to be somewhere
else.
        There was also in this world

a metronome which served as overseer
of the time-space continuum, a regulator
of the so to speak *basso continuo* of existence.
The metronome was unaware that he in turn
was overseen by a higher power, a man
named Wolfgang Amadeus Mozart. Mozart
was a child who had the physical appearance
of a genius, so that when he appeared
in public great sheets of light ripped
from his presence and flew away. One such
sheet wrapped itself around a bird so
that the bird was shot through with
this light.
          The villagers noticed a bright
object in the sky at night, moving about
unlike stars or moon or other celestial bodies,
and they soon created stories to explain
this phenomenon. You see, they were unable
to see Mozart: he had been dead
for over 200 years. But his death was the kind
that remains over the years that pass,
not under them. He was buried in the sky,
and if you'll recall what I told you
about the time-space continuum you'll understand
just what I mean. Anyway,
one explanation of the gliding brightness
in the night sky was that some electricity
from a bolt of lightning had been captured
inside an idea which had lost the mind
it came from. Others felt that some sticks
had caught fire.
Neither of these theories was true, although
the sticks idea is interesting: the bird
could die, decompose, fertilize a small tree,
and go into the limbs which then
would fall or be torn from the tree,
set alight, and cast into the air.
The second movement of the arm that cast them,
the downward movement, the arm
attached to the body of Mozart

as he composed his Serenade No. 11,
the downward movement, I say, terminates
in a delicate flutter of the wrist and fingers,
and the cuckoo bird alights on a branch.
It sits there for a moment, sensing.
Once again the arm rises. The bird pours forth
a song which the Japanese felt sounded
like *hototogisu,* which is Japanese
for "cuckoo," whereas we think it sounds
like "cuckoo." The fact that both cultures
are correct illustrates my point
about the time-space continuum.
Actually the *hototogisu* and cuckoo are
different birds, but I equate them
to demonstrate a point. But back to our story.
First let me explain that the villagers'
first explanation, of electricity trapped
inside an idea which had lost the mind it came from,
would have been true had they not carelessly
sought to explain everything by electricity.
"Electricity" was a word they used
at random, a catch-all meaning virtually nothing.
Electrical concepts had permeated their religion
the way atoms permeated matter in the twentieth century:
so small as to be everything
once you got the idea. The idea
the villagers had was correct insofar
as they linked the mysterious nocturnal illumination
to a mental being, to, of course,
none other than Mozart. He is in
this room with me right now, not
figuratively speaking: he quite
literally is in this room, his real physical person.
He is signing a contract which will
grant me all rights to his works past,
present, and future. Actually this is a part
of the story I should have reserved for later,
and about how he is deaf, dumb, blind, and paralyzed
from the toes up. Yes, time has taken
its dreadful toll of the great composer, even.

Think of the men who dragged great stones
over vast deserts, only to hurl them
into deep chasms! Great stones
which diminish in size as they fall,
clattering like small hailstones
as they hit the canyon floor, where Handel
scoops them into a basket. Back
in his cave he affixes stems to them;
if only he had a staff to place them on!
Instead he must fling them into the air
and watch them increase in size, only
to fall back. Of course some notes did
continue to rise from time to time:
The Harmonious Blacksmith is one example,
notes that go so high up they become planets.
Incidentally, the planets of the solar system,
arranged on a circular staff around the sun,
form the basis of Couperin's *Pièces
de Clavecin,* but perceived as
the "music of the spheres" not in two dimensions
but in three: this "natural" music being
more complete than "written" music,
which is flat, pardon the pun. The great beauty
of man's "written" music consists in its complete removal
from anything we think of as "real," in fact
it is very much like the word "real" itself:
once said it becomes utterly without meaning.
But this digression goes on too long: my story
concerns the single and remarkable meeting of
Wolfgang Amadeus Mozart (1756-1791) and George Frideric
      Handel (1685-1759).
You will notice that Mozart was three when Handel died,
or so musical history tells us. The truth
of the matter is that Handel did not die
until the autumn of 1786, when he not only
met the young Mozart but actually
collaborated with him on an operetta in one act,
Bastien und Bastienne, K. 50, a piece commissioned
by Dr. Anton Mesmer, the discoverer of animal magnetism.
Mesmer was a perverted homosexual who attempted

to use his discovery for evil ends:
he tried to hypnotize young Viennese boys.
He was successful in the case of Mozart; in fact
Mozart wrote his part of *Bastien und Bastienne*
under hypnosis. Handel was of course a notorious
homosexual in his own time, but was well
beyond his prime by 1768. He refused to submit
to hypnotic suggestion and in fact was unaware
that the young Mozart was "in Mesmer's power."
The premiere of *Bastien und Bastienne* took place
in the open-air theater of Mesmer's house
in the suburbs of Vienna, with Mesmer directing
the production and playing Bastienne. In
his perversity he cast the by then ancient
Anna Maria Strada del Po, the exceptionally ugly
opera star whom Londoners had nicknamed "The Pig,"
in the role of Bastien. Colas was played
by a someone who drifted back
into the forever mists of the Unknown.

  Mesmer, an insanely jealous man, suspecting
that Handel was about to steal his young lover,
devised a monstrous plan which culminated
in having Handel bound and gagged, carted
onto the stage near the end of the sixth scene,
and as Bastienne sang

   O Lust, o Lust
   Für die entflammte Brust!

   O Joy! O Joy!
   For the burning breast!

he set fire to the venerable composer.
The light-hearted pastoral continued
with no one's taking notice: Mozart under
hypnosis, Anna Maria Strada del Po a hopeless
senile and opium addict, and the audience
a bizarre group of statuary assembled
by Mesmer from all over the world.

My Coup

The bright light of what could be an electric angel hits my face head-on, a light into which I am asked, as it were, to step and speak. Actually I've just stepped into it, and I'm now speaking: my mouth is saying one thing and my brain is thinking another. The mouth is that of an imaginary head attached to a real body standing at a podium on those wide steps on Kreshchatik, the main street in Kiev. Behind and above me wave the bright red flags that sprang from the blood of Lenin. The crowd before me has turned their faces up to the sky to watch the angel flitting back and forth, like a leaf dancing in the wind, a leaf that should be at the top of a Christmas tree. Their ears hear only the vibrations from the angel's hospital gown as it flaps contrapuntually with the red flags. I give out a sigh of relief and step down from the podium. Now I can go back home to my window and wife, and gaze out at the little yellow bird that comes to the windowsill almost every morning.

Poem

When I am dead and gone
they will say of me,
"We never could figure out
what he was talking about,
but it was clear that he
understood very well
that modernism is a branch
that was cut off decades ago."
Guess who said that.
Mutt and Jeff
who used to look so good
in the comics.
I especially liked their mustaches.
And the sense in it
that God is watching
from some untelevised height,
and sometimes

throws himself on the ground.
There is a tremendous impact,
for the molecules of God
are just tremendous.

Essay on Imagination

So I go to the baseball stadium. It is large, larger than I had thought
it would be, and it is surprisingly fast, moving along at about forty
miles per hour. At this rate we will be playing Saint Louis by morn-
ing! By a stroke of good fortune, I happen to be the only person on
the promenade deck, a real treat. The smooth green expanse of field
before me is, for this moment, all mine. Am I dreaming, I ask my-
self. The answer is no, you are not dreaming, you are having a fan-
tasy that you are at a baseball stadium that is also an ocean liner. The
answer makes me slump deeper into my personality, the part I sleep
in, and so I get sleepy. If I go to sleep, I can dream about the ball
field, and what might have happened there as we crossed the ocean,
me and the blond girl who has just arrived, wearing black shorts that
are cut achingly high in the back and a black bandanna across her
chest, and as she mounts the stairs with a drowsy rolling of her hips
I realize that she is a composite of all the girls I've ever glimpsed in
the street with that pang of fleeting lust that glows for a moment
and fades away into me and then rolls back out, because the power
of the imagination cannot be contained, no matter how hard we try.

Sleep Alarm

Just as some guy
is proposing to
Suzanne Pleshette in a cough
syrup commercial,
I realize
I've dozed back off and snap
to, crack my left
eye and see you,
dog formed
by shadows of art
books along the wall.

Prose Poem

The morning coffee. I'm not sure why I drink it. Maybe it's the ritual of the cup, the spoon, the hot water, the milk, and the little heap of brown grit, the way they come together to form a nail I can hang the day on. It's something to do between being asleep and being awake. Surely there's something better to do, though, than to drink a cup of instant coffee. Such as meditate? About what? About having a cup of coffee. A cup of coffee whose first drink is too hot and whose last drink is too cool, but whose many in-between drinks are, like Baby Bear's porridge, just right. Papa Bear looks disgruntled. He removes his spectacles and swivels his eyes onto the cup that sits before Baby Bear, and then, after a discrete cough, reaches over and picks it up. Baby Bear doesn't understand this disruption of the morning routine. Papa Bear brings the cup close to his face and peers at it intently. The cup shatters in his paw, explodes actually, sending fragments and brown liquid all over the room. In a way it's good that Mama Bear isn't there. Better that she rest in her grave beyond the garden, unaware of what has happened to the world.

Euphues

I dunno about this *Euphues.*
Lyly's language is gorgeous,
of course, occasionally irritating,
too, so you feel satisfied
to have the experience just
behind you. You get up and go outside
and have a hot dog in the sunlight and
think about the conjunctions,
those pinions
that allow our sentences to rotate in mid-course:
"The afternoon was mild, although not yet over,"
placing the dependent clause in direct opposition
to the main clause, like a woman who suddenly
turns to face you and it takes
your breath away—there is a moment
of silence and intensity—the boats
are frozen on the bay and no little doggie barks.

"I've been meaning to say something to you…,"
she begins. And your heart
sinks: something massive
is about to happen,
you will be joined to this woman
by a tremendous force, something like
gravity, in which
hats float down onto our heads and we smile.
    We smile toward this countess of Pembroke
with her delicate lips and translation
of *The Psalms* with her brother Sir Philip Sydney,
the great poet and of the great tradition of
fine comportment. His conjunctions
were in perfect order
and he exuded a harmony,
a tone actually heard in the air.

Song

Little violet,
all alone,
stem curved,
quiet zone.

Little snowdrops,
clustered, white,
patchy ground,
frozen night.

Little hawkweed,
casual, fierce,
sunny friend,
I like you.

Little daisy,
meadow's edge,
loose wind,
the world a stage.

Black-eyed Susan,
Spanish lass,
drowsy gestures,
long eyelash.

Gentian yodel,
clear blue,
dignified,
gentle lake.

Wild rose,
"I don't care,"
you're nonchalant,
crimson flare.

Pink clover,
home for tea,
do come in,
be like me.

Goldenrod,
drift in breeze,
catch a nose,
make it sneeze.

Daffodil,
crazy duck,
trumpet searching,
nice colors.

Velvet pansy,
ruffled cheeks,
jets of jet,
lie down on me.

Clean geranium,
nurse's aid,
red and green,
bills are paid.

Buttercup!
of yellow butter,
chubby kid
just like his mother.

Joe Brainard's Painting "Bingo"

I suffer when I sit next to Joe Brainard's painting "Bingo"

I could have made that line into a whole stanza

I suffer
When I sit
Next to Joe
Brainard's painting
"Bingo"

Or I could change the line arrangement

I suffer when I sit

That sounds like hemorrhoids
I don't know anything about hemorrhoids
Such as if it hurts to sit when you have them
If so I must not have them
Because it doesn't hurt me to sit
I probably sit about $^8/_{15}$ of my life

Also I don't suffer
When I sit next to Joe Brainard

Actually I don't even suffer
When I sit next his painting "Bingo"
Or for that matter any of his paintings

In fact I didn't originally say
I suffer when I sit next to Joe Brainard's painting "Bingo"
My wife said it
In response to something I had said
About another painting of his
She had misunderstood what I had said

Tone Arm

The clouds go rolling over
The rooftops of the 17th
18th or 19th century buildings–
They are really rolling

You people of the future
How I hate you
You are alive and I'm not
I don't care whether you read my poetry or not

      I.

The diamond is real—
See how it cusses over the pheasant
A kind of test lad
Who kicked the elevated man on the bag of light
When just ahead a kind of gold foil geometry
Was spread across a time lapse of London

The results of that experiment came later
Since now you know its diction
Just up here come here

The thin family will die out
When the swans on the ornamental lake
Are signaled
By the French Revolution

Sentence the tattered bucket spinning of the tree

What's all this talk about
Law and order
I wish you would go stick your head up your own butt
As well as your hands, feet, midriff, and other parts
I'm sick of you you turd-faced queer

Well
This town ain't very big at sundown
And the other Henry is approaching
The dusky ski
Which is penetrating your heart at this moment

For what is art but a bauble
On the breast of Time
Or the lady that gives you the time

I'd like to cough on the breast
Of the lady who gives me the time
Arta longa vita brevis

It's a codpiece that I brought along this here vitamin boat
Where you and I
The two of us
Can dilly and dally the whole day through
With naught a thought
But of me and of you
Trouble is
You are a sullen dart

I warned you
You should never have come
But now that you're here I may as well tell you everything
About the orb
A man saw a ball of gold

Later

What is this anyway
But a sort of alchemy of the mouse
Who enters and exits from
His little house

New York. March 8 (RP)–
This will be man's greatest accomplishment
Hand in the old night

up the de Kooning

Whose sullen felicitation now emits
A sort of deafening knob
You turn to get to an "in"
Sign

I salute you, jigsaw critters of the Northwest
But please leave this wafer to another
Dram in the presence of a craw

After a fashion
All breathed easier
Through their own noses
Your nose for instance

I've seen many a ruble in my day
But none so fugitive as this one
You have offered me
As a consolation for being the local
Anesthetic of "I warned you, Brett"

You may wish to lock me out of your life forever
Or to live as a lock lives
On the bean of understanding
A mole's destruction of the weathery facts
We all pretend are true–
By the way, signore, they are all true

By the sea
I remember you when I met you
There by the stately sea, the sea
That is both stately and wholly of itself
Your wings resembled arms
Your beak was as if a woman's mouth
Or a man's that resembled an entire woman
Now I understand that you were a man
Dressed as a bird
One wishes to Ernst upon
To feel the nitrogen and mustard guts
    ….ah!
Your muscles are bands of steel! and your beak
Emits a country-and-western-style song

Go away, glib cur
You were not made for poesy
You aspire, how shall I say, too much?

Token

  2.

I used to know a song about a hamper
It went
"On a large sock, O…."

The rind of Borneo
Is absolutely zero zero
An etude!

Adjourn the cup is pure

Is it perfect if I rip off your sandals
And bring them to you

A dress retreating
Through a forest fire makes another whole sense

Unfortunately and I'm sorry
I forgot the star of the show
I can see it all now

      3.

Some showdowns are shaping up   the crude limbs of history
And if the definitions are just   a bunch of shit
Step the other way   deftly!
Avoiding the good car

I was just walking in the street in a short-sleeve shirt
This man passes me going the other way
He was going the other way!

Everything
Needs an intermission
Since in these days here and there
There's not much
One can get many little pleasures from

Wood
Fire   Not that I mind going up
Air   In this ace of hearts
Water

He pulled out his giant prick etc.

He?
Who?
Who did?

Some people came to visit me in prison
They said I was going to pieces
But the person they came to be
Took the rest of the stickers away   (*He hands them to her.*)

I suppose we're worth more these days
Pulling out our giant pricks
My friend Joe Brainard wants to sell his body to a medical school

I feel the whole world shaking
Something must be going on
One never knew, dear, oh dear
The shortness of your answers
Would contribute to this sergeant feeling of sadness
That tugs at my ears
On the clean spring days that are going on around me
My mother, my father, and my friends

            4.

Let's take a string quartet
Playing one of Beethoven's compositions
We may explain it as the scratching
Of a horse's hair against a cat's gut;
Or we may explain it as the mind
Of a genius soaring up to an infinite
Horse's hair scratching against an infinite cat's gut

            5.

Hasten the chinchilla
For tonight you die

Only a clever ruse extends the wastebasket
Wise men are said to keep
This weather makes no difference is pure information
Rain banging the toes

            6.

A red car rolls out.
You are the closely pursued prey of a pack of cards,

Or a parcel of fish.
You are, in fact, a slip
Of the tongue drifting to the point of no return.
But you do return this time
As a child trampled by a rabbit.
A red hat burns in the feces about
Which you are led towards an object
Made of ropes and spikes–an instrument.
And you are also the one who lies thirsting near
The edge of the cog, yet cannot reach it with your mouth.
Then you hit the dust off the record
Changing everything.

7.

What modern poetry needs
Is a good beating
It is the love call of the gorilla
And a knob is born stunningly

On the affirmative plaza
Huge crowds affirm
An affirming machine

There is indeed money in the tummy
Though wisecracks split the ocean
Throwing up a bad leather pellet
You reach for a vegetable
The train is accountably wrecking

But I know
I'll never bring back that awful stick again
To beat you mercifully
Grandma

8.

In its own little place near the obviously phony barn
The spirit evaporates like wise cows before a farmer
In the dawn decorated with mist
Warming up
The day's delicate experiences

Death waits at the end of the trail
And he's boss
O who will lay him out with a good right cross
(Religion, do your part)

I wish (toot toot) to eat it and make beautiful music
Together sometime but not right now
You can have your old city environment, though
With its words on boulevards
I want to walk on a wounded leg in fine weather

9.

One makes mistakes in order to appear
Before the human race does

Another poop scene: the last
We see of you
Is this pathetic little figure selling olives

Why do you attack the door, aggressive penny?
Because the scissors you left behind
Snip narcotically at a small thing in a cup

Or
The painter's name was interesting–to be precise,
Rather interesting.

10.

You have a lovely name-calling instinct
Though some say you stink
Or so you think
Ted to the high heavens
For even the gravest accents trip occasionally
Through fields of wheat, slaw, and a third
Where desolation's grape snuggles closer to
Desolation's other grapes, forming
An excellent, a piercing arrangement

As they do
So do we
These squeeks emerge from scissor-holes

Causing a gentle motion in the eardrums
No, I have nothing to declare
But your country is beautiful
It wishes to stay here

Poinsettia ravages automobile
Subjecting it to summer's gentle torture

The taxi is beautiful because it is open at all hours
Said George Washington Carver
Whose head shall be separated from his body forever more
He went to Chicago in a taxi
Not the Chicago of Sandburg
But the Chicago of tissue and how to get there
Am I disturbing you?
It's wonderful, splendid!
To put one's foot in a Wednesday night rape
You see I am bored
In fact, I am short of money
Here comes winter's dim claw (balance)

II.

Batten down the hatches boys I'm having an idea!
It was cold, very cold....
(What is a house
But a bunch of hints thrown
In and out a window?
This suggests that history
O infinite hints!
Has sometime in its past
Caught up with itself
Come by itself
Passé
Is now only an imitation of itself
Like a car
Driving toward itself in the rain
Developing its own misty personality
Only to be photographed from behind
As we all eventually are.

In other words a house

I suppose
May as well be a horse's ass
Breaking the visible chains of logic.

12.

Outside my window is preparing for the darkness
That broke my mother's heart—
For you kiss a pair of lips only to realize,
Later, that it was a single lip, in fact
The Blarney Stone.... You see how lucky you really are
Though the bicycle part is over
The fence first. The size of the buildings
You step over is of no importance
Since the buildings brought their own sky,
One you enjoyed but preferred to run
Like a funny baby into

13.

The Jews like to eat
The Italians like to eat
The Irish like to drink
The Germans like to think
The French, they like to swim
And sink and swim
MY ANIMALS

14.

For one brings everything to a bear
In a crucial moment
On a silver platter—or better yet
A silver spoon whose engraving tells
Of a future

The bear holds a jerking fish in his dumb paw;
In fact, he is standing on his hind legs, and
Judging from this equally bad drawing,
The legs of other bears as well.
That's what it's always been, hasn't it?

From book to bed to book
With nothing but perfect holes between,
Spaces to be filled in later
Or simply brought out as in invisible ink
As the case may be, as
A hammer is brought down as you move toward the bed
A book in one hand a book in the other
Both feet moving, one then the other.
Yes, something is moving toward the bed
As surely as day and night flip through one another
Like a ball.
What might be
Is of no concern to me—
You see I have neither tooth nor brain in my head,
Which love conspires
To relieve you of.

15.

He went for an empty holster.
A short circuit was blamed.
It was a musical score.
Try the packet.
And his pants—that's France.

16.

Socrates was a mutt, this is generally not known
But understood at some hilarious fork
For a few years! oh
Then watch the ducks peck at gunpowder on the dental walks
Where we pace so as not to upset the tipping lake

Now the ducks are picketing the island
We can get to
The hills (those hills) pose instead and offer themselves
We climb the hellish peanut
Now the ducks are standing in a white surface

The grassy edges rise to music's flown cough
Now the ducks tear the water's surface off

The telling ducks
The park is moving out
Now the ducks cornered in sunset are really burning up
Now the ducks assault the night they're turning away from

O but we could throw down sects
And step on it

17.

Sir
Will you please keep going to the bathroom you do it magnificently
Which reminds me
Of this place, this time, you and me
We're back!
We are eating terrific amounts of food
Food food
So we can go to the bathroom good good good

You're weak I'm not
Your
Energy gone down someone else's cheek's rosy sheet
I'm quite comfortable here
In my motorized chair
That was crated by mistake
Those tears could take you miles up
To the rosy heavens we thought so wonderful just a little while ago
Don't I know it

I can't help it, Louis, Louis Pasteur
Deft chemist of manure
It's back again that pastille you hated so

18.

The genitals run amock
Sliding in and out and around one another
It's really quite a show
And here I have two beautiful young girls in this room
Both of whom I am going to fuck unmercifully
These girls that skim along a beach of money

Let's say we look
Into this box and
See two ladies talking
With one another. Each
Is standing on a beach.
The lady on the left....

Several peaceful girls come running down the beach
But the letters they are fly away
Like gentle, harmless farts

Those girls I spoke of there
Were hit only here and there
With bright patches of color
They had no bodies
Please do not think of them as the products of a vivid imagination

Right now I just happen to be looking at the Atlantic Ocean
Or at least a part of it
Please to box with me on the beach?

The white pellet passes under the monster
Decorating the fence
Down the fence goes the pellet
Then becomes the pellet of distance
Which is what it always was anyway

Old kinds of geometry are strafing the beach
In search of this famous belly
Perhaps it is the pellet they are searching for
Or the hole made in the sky
By the pellet bye and bye

If I had the world's great grease extinct beside me now
I could at last kill
The people who go out and drop carelessly into the holes
Of the white pinball machine
They tally, yes
But without the ho!
And when you add up the scores
Generosity erases them
After all

19.

In guarded spasms you broke the ruler
Vanishing 7
Good heavens! was said

The fact broke the cigarette too
And that mad us
Or the other version of the clink at Columbia University

The clink that falls fiery off the bridge
Over the large canyon
The climate that day was contest though
Crowds disperse. Girls bleed in the great calm

20.

You select something small like a pimple
And quick as a wink that's all there is
In a world of moles, pores, hairs, and other
Indications are made
Who made them?
Not you, certainly, but the lonely pimple
On its journey to the tip of the nose
Which is its destiny
This blemish you see
Is a stage unto itself
And also around itself
One on which you perform
For you are smaller than the smallest pimple
When smoke goes rushing over the vase

When the vase goes rushing over the ocean
I'll be rushing with it
Toward native lands
To take a shower along with me
Dismantling the atmosphere with my hands

21.

Sings

When the cows and the leaves begin to fall
They fall like falsehood

Just as coffee comes from the brains
Well-behaved elephants pass

Sandpaper toughens the holes
The dialogues of Plato rage in the pre-dawn

The wind shows off
The cows fall again

The bus goes pitching over Kansas
Joe is reading
I am asleep

I wired the violets

§

A contact lens drifts above the cervix
And it's not a bad idea

You work in a highly visible bowl

22.

"I'm coaching in the orange groves
Near the snow fields of my heart"
Is an example of a kind of poetry
I wish to discuss here. It is not
Simply great poetry nor is it simply
Great sentiment, it is both.

23.

You go on as a taxicab keeping still to this music
Me, I do my homework

Hashish go
Under your dress… at the dining room table
All suspect.
              And you tsk
the Pied Piper, 6 foot 4.

–Classic January black–
Prince P. broke the light on the porch

Where used to run and play the glass figure
That is no more!

24.

I am shaving in the distance
The nights come and pass by
Come and pass by
There is a tremendous nature here
Where I am
A shirt is here, too

First Drift

The writing of poems
and the living of life
seem to require
paying hard attention
to any and everything,
and experiencing
a kind of mental orgasm.
Yikes! Do I
mean that?
Unfortunately, I'm afraid
I did, dipped to scoop
an idea from the roadside,
the mental roadside that runs
alongside the mental highway
that leads to a mental hospital.
I have never been a patient
in a mental hospital, because
I think it would be an extremely bad place to be.
So I stay out.
And stay home.
And go down the street,
looking intently at everything.
Sometimes the people in the street
laugh and turn into sheet music
torn from the sky and left to flutter down

into the metaphor that hides behind the deity,
and will not show itself,
like a basement beneath the ocean,
with a tree that grew through a sheet of glass
on which your face was painted,
like a clown's, in the early morning
when it was just starting to rain
and the animals are moving, and the tents
are rippling in the breeze, and inside Glenda
the chimpanzee is completing a quadruple somersault
from shining bar to shining bar.

The Fortune Cookie Man

Working for ten years now at the fortune cookie factory and I'm still
not allowed to write any of the fortunes. I couldn't do any worse
than they do, what with their You Will Find Success in the Enter-
tainment Field mentality. I would like to tell someone that they will
find a gorilla in their closet, brooding darkly over the shoes. And
that that gorilla will roll his glassy, animal eyes as if to cry out to the
heavens that are burning in bright orange and red and through
which violent clouds are rolling, and open his beast's mouth and
issue a whimper that will fall on the shoes like a buffing rag hot with
friction. But they say no. So if you don't find success in the enter-
tainment field, don't blame me. I just work here.

Ode to Bohemians

I.

The stars at night
Are big and bright
The moon above
A pale blue dove

The trees bent out
By windy shout
Of West Wind god
And the soldiers bolted from their ranks

—Did they O did they?—
And spilled across the countryside,
ants escaping some ant doom,
the final trumpet from the god of ant death...
while their wives were waiting in the kitchen doorway
in red aprons and yellow bandannas,
really beautiful little black ants....

    2.

Two eyes bulging out with red lines
and rolling upon the ground...
all the better to see you with,
microscopic weakling!
You rush below the microscopes of government,
the government of Russia, the government of the U.S.A.,
the horrible governments of Argentina and Brazil, the suspicious
governments of Greece, Venezuela, and Turkey,
the governments strong and weak, a few weird bigshots
making you eat dirt and like it, buddy.
For me, I say, "Fuck it."
I have a glass of red wine
and a beret upon my head,
I am tipsy in Montmartre,
my smock smeared with paint
and the lipstick of script girls,
and I salute zees life I lead,
O happy vagabond! O stalwart bohemian,
defying the ordinary rules of society
to express your inner self,
to tell those callous motherfuckers
what it's like, to achieve
the highest glory of man
and then sink back in its clouds
never to be seen again, like strange celebrities
whose caricatures
grow dim and fade
from the pages of memory. Thank you, anyway
you colorful individuals.

Blacktop

The newly blacktopped highway with the bright yellow stripe down the middle slides under and behind you like a deep carpet as you whiz toward home in the silent and starry night, but deep inside the motor the pistons are incredibly hot and intense, and the noise is terrible, and the sparkplugs are spitting little zaps of electricity like crazy—and all for you, movie-goers laughing on your way home.

Famous Flames

With all my faults
I do have one virtue:
I respect the idea of the noble book.
(No kidding!)
I take seriously the works of Aristotle,
although I do not usually like them.
I take seriously the *Tao Teh Ching*
and I always bark like a dog,
with the gray silhouette of a factory
against a deep red sky
and it is the France of Zola,
he whose high heels clicked
against a marble bust of Pallas.
These gentlemen are very interesting.
Take Montaigne. A peculiar guy, and
very interesting. Or Spinoza,
he of the face ugly
and geometry as divinity.
He looked in the mirror and said, "Ouch!"
and he looked into the ouch
and saw a perfect circle.
A leads to B and to C
and that explains the universe!
Unfortunately that face belonged to René Descartes!

Me, I bit into the coleslaw
and killed the dragon where he breathed
funny fumes on the pages of Literature.

"I am Everyman."
What a funny thing to say!
Would a tree say, "I am tree"?
I do not think so,
I do not think so just yet.

An ominous sensation steals over the back
as though a magnetic field
were searching, vaguely,
for another magnetic field.
Card players, in marathon games,
smoking Camels, have claimed
to have seen visions, one
in which the Virgin Mary came down
out of the sky and gave him the three of spades.
Others believe they can change the pips
by force of mind, as the card flies through the air,
and it's your open.
You sit at the present moment
with the future ready to welcome you,
until the bubble bursts
and the crowds begin to move again.
It is Christmas, 1944. The man
who invented the question mark
was laughing in heaven. Human beings
had turned into exclamation points
that threw skinny shadows across the earth
as it turned in space lit only by an old flashlight.
It was a pretty cheap production,
and when Tommy entered it in the science fair
Mr. Bushwhanger was embarrassed.
He ran and banged his head
against the wall of the faculty lounge
until his glasses fell on the floor,
burst into flame.

Love Poem

We have plenty of matches in our house.
We keep them on hand always.
Currently our favorite brand is Ohio Blue Tip,
though we used to prefer Diamond brand.
That was before we discovered Ohio Blue Tip matches.
They are excellently packaged, sturdy
little boxes with dark and light blue and white labels
with words lettered on the shape of a megaphone,
as if to say even louder to the world,
"Here is the most beautiful match in the world,
its one and a half inch soft pine stem capped
by a grainy dark purple head, so sober and furious
and stubbornly ready to burst into flame,
lighting, perhaps, the cigarette of the woman you love,
for the first time, and it was never really the same
after that. All this will we give you."
That is what you gave me, I
become the cigarette and you the match, or I
the match and you the cigarette, blazing
with kisses that smolder toward heaven.

A Man Saw a Ball of Gold

A man saw a ball of gold in the sky;
He climbed for it,
And eventually he achieved it–
It was gold.

Now this is the strange part:
When the man went to the earth
And looked again,
Lo, there was the ball of gold.
Now this is the strange part:
It was a ball of gold.
Ay, by the heavens, it was a ball of gold.

Ode to Stupidity

1.

Duh… I… uh…
I bet you never heard of Huntz Hall!
Huntz, he was a heck of a guy!
He had two eyes, in his head!
And a mouth, under them!
And some other stuff, like you know
Ears and stuff, but the best
Was his brains, boy did that guy
Have brains! I saw him do great stuff
One day in the movie theater, he
Was on the screen with his friend Leo
And they were in trouble and Huntz
Got them out of this trouble and
Ever since then I've been a changed man.
You might describe it as a pivotal experience
In my personal life, crucial, at any rate.
The jaws of a big pair of pliers
Are gripping the edge of my desk–
I have learned how to make them do this!
And when I go out into the street
My leg is special–just one leg, I
haven't learned to make two legs special.

2.

Dawn breaks over the sprawling metropolis,
You drink a glass of beer at three o'clock,
Friends come and they go, the post office
Refuses a package, girls lie down
And are fucked by huge turtles, a voice is heard,
The dictionary is opened to page 387
By a young man who pores over the entry
For "hermetic": eye wanders to "heroic":
"Fix'd is the Term to all the Race of Earth,
And such the hard Condition of our Birth"
And a green and orange carton is discarded.

Perception and cognition arrange these bits and pieces
Into a recognizable pattern which, associated
With feelings, forms a continuity
Which is our life. Yes, there are jagged
Edges here and there, huge spaces
Ripped out by intruding gizmos wielded
By gigantic Skeezixes who come to fix gigantic gizmos,
But generally it is more like the River Thames,
Smoothly flowing, punctuated by boats
Where people raise their smiling faces and wave
To you, women overheard yesterday
Who said today would be cold and it is warm,
You thought you would feel bad this morning
And you do not but the street
Looks chewed up, people lose their footing,
Their mouths open in surprise as they slip and fall,
Perhaps some old person will break their hip!
So you examine the street, write a letter,
Organize a march, run for Congress, lead
A revolution, are stood before a firing squad
Without a cigarette dangling between your lips!
They didn't even give you a cigarette!
No cigarette!
And as a final mockery to your ideals,
The assassins are smoking four cigarettes each,
Billows of smoke pouring from their faces,
Vision obscured, so that when their rifles
Expel the bullets, chickens
Fall from the sky, 39 cents per pound!
And you are liberated by a band of *campesinos*
In white pyjamas who then melt back
Into the wall some bullets had knocked chips from,
Liberated too from your social conscience
Or love of country, but still a wounded figure
Who hides back up in the hills, counting the days
Before he will sprout wings, like Hermes',
And fly with his message through space and time.

Homage to Max Jacob

Goodbye sting and all my columbines
In the tower which looks out gently
Their yo-yo plumage on the cold bomb shoulder
      Goodbye sting

Goodbye house and its little blue roofs
Where such a friend in all seasons
To see us again made some money
      Goodbye house

Goodbye line of hay in pigs
Near the clock! O! how often I hurt myself
That you know me like an apartment
      Goodbye line!

Goodbye lamb grease! hands carrying arteries
On the well-varnished little park mirror
Of white barricades the color of diapers
      Goodbye lamb grease!

Goodbye verges calves and planks
And on the sting of our black flying boat
Our servant with her white hair-do
      Goodbye verges

Goodbye my clear oval river
Goodbye mountain! Goodbye cherry trees!
It is you who are my cap and tale
      Not Paris

Flower's Escape

What have we here, a little daisy alongside the footpath, hmm. But
as I bend to pick it, I pause, I freeze, I am a statue, and the daisy ex-
pands to the height of a man and begins to move off down the foot-
path, barely skimming the ground, its petals flared back in the
breeze. But I don't mind. Being immobile like this will give me time
to contemplate the eternity that lies before me, and whose silent
voice insists on reminding me, from time to time, "Ron, you are

not." Sometimes this happens when I've gone to bed and am lying there suddenly aware of how dark it is in the room; sometimes it happens when I'm driving along a country road, a ghost in my pickup truck! And I think how funny it is that I, who am not, am also a man driving a red truck, and the flexibility of my body is enjoying itself as I wind up and take the curves in a gentle centrifugal arc and my body weighs a little more on that side for a moment, and Nat "King" Cole is telling me I'm unforgettable, which I appreciate, although I know full well that I will be forgotten, unless I stay like this, bent over a flower that has fled my touch.

High Heels

I have a vision
in my head of Cubism
and Constructivism
in all their artistic purity
joined with a decorative attractiveness
that exceeds deliciousness,
even more to be desired
than becoming a milkman
in a white suit and hat
delivering milk to the back door
of a white frame house
on a street lined with elms
and being invited inside
by the curvaceous, translucent lady
of the house, not once
but many times, too many times,
perhaps, for later her husband
will be coming home
with a sledgehammer in his hand,
the pink hand with light blue fingernails, oh
you have colored the wrong picture!
You were to put the pink and blue
on the beachball on the next page.

With Lee Remick at Midnight

The lights shoot off the windows of the Plaza
and into the sky where they become stars.

Stars shine over the Playa de Toros
in Mexico, D.F.

We have a Washington, D.C.
We have such a thing as alternating current.

The current flows in one direction for a while
And then in the opposite, alternating rapidly thus.

I get up out of my chair and walk to one end of the room.
There I see a little statue of a friend, Tony Towle.

Hat, coat, muffler, and gloves appear on the statue
As the door closes overhead and the sky is black.

My hand reaches for the alarm clock in a dawn
Muddle-headed wha? and I settle into another level

Of being. I want to read Marx, *The Voyage of the Beagle,*
Jean-Jacques Rousseau and Thomas Jefferson, get out

Of bed and meet Bob by noon to have
Mousse au chocolat chez Schrafft's

And be back home in time to hear Fred Flintstone
Give out his mysterious "Yabba-dabba-dooo!" wahoo,

As evening settles down in its glorious space
And I shoot down the slide and up, and out

Olivetti Lettera

Goodbye, little Lettera.
It was nice with you again.
I once loved a girl and oh
Well I once loved a girl.

You are so small, the way

what I remember is
packed into my human skull
and it's dark in there.

And it's singing in there,
this typewriter who is a
girl, then, an Italian girl,
undressing, slowly, in the dark.

Reading Reverdy

The wind that went through the head left it plural.

      .

The half-erased words on the wall of bread.

      .

Someone is grinding the color of ears.
She looks like and at her.

      .

A child draws a man and the earth
Is covered with snow.

      .

He comes down out of the night
When the hills fall.

      .

The line part of you goes out to infinity.

      .

I get up on top of an inhuman voice.

Poema del City

I live in the city.
It's a tough life,
often unpleasant, sometimes
downright awful. But it has what
we call its compensations.

To kill a roach, for example,
is to my mind not pleasant
but it does develop one's reflexes.

Wham!
and that's that.
Sometimes, though, the battered roach
will haul itself onto broken legs and,
wildly waving its bent antennae,
stagger off into the darkness

to warn the others, who live in the shadow
of the great waterfall in their little teepees.
Behind them rise the gleaming brown and blue mass
of the Grand Tetons, topped with white snow
that blushes, come dawn, and glows, come dusk.
Silent gray wisps rise from the smoldering campfires.

Poema del City 2

A light chill on the knees
& I sneeze
up late, alone, in my house, winter
rain against the window and glittering there
in the constant light from stoops across the street
cars hiss down from one moment to
the next hour: in an hour
I'll be asleep. Wrapped
in new sheets and old quilts
with my wife warm beside me and my son
asleep in the next room, I'll
be so comfortable and dreamy, so happy
I'm not terribly damaged or dying yet
but sailing, secure, secret and all
those other peaceful *s*'s fading
like warm taillights down a long landscape
with no moon at all.
                    Ah, it's sweet,
this living, to make you cry, or rise
& sneeze, and douse the light.

After the Broken Arm

From point A a wind is blowing to point B
Which is here, where the pebble is only a mountain.
If truly heaven and earth are out there
Why is that man waving his arms around,
Gesturing to the word "lightning" written on the clouds
That surround and disguise his feet?

If you say the right word in New York City
Nothing will happen in New York City.
But out in the fabulous dry horror of the West
A beautiful girl named Sibyl will burst
In by the open window breathless
And settle for an imaginary glass of something.
But now her name is no longer Sibyl—it's Herman,
Yearning for point B.

Dispatch this note to our hero at once.

Wilson '57

A terrific blast:
stately white columns sunk in deep fog
and the face of Miss Sheehan enshrined in soft focus
above a crisp Mr. Elstner at his neat desk, ready to work,
shadow flashed onto the wall,
his face a living reprimand; then
Miss Helen G. Lee, Miss Giffert, Mrs. (!) Craig, class
counselors all, their old ladies' forties mashed curls
shimmering in studio light, their expressions a mixture
of benevolent understanding and acerb malevolence.
One day Larry Bennett stood up in Social Studies
and said in his soprano voice, "Miss Lee,
I think you are stupid." I'll never remember
the bland faces of the Office Workers, glued
to their typewriters but friendly withal. Here troops
of individuals are scattered over the steps, standing,
others sedately seated, some in contrapposto poses,
others caught yawning, surprised, blinking, blank,

utterly frozen, hardened in Revlon. "You've been
a very nice student–good luck! Mrs. Plunkett"
whom students called "The Frog"
to commemorate her hideous face.
Rex Stith, unjustly renamed Stiff, is casually friendly
and elected President. Bill Vanburkleo, more athletic
but less executive, achieves the Vice-Presidency.
Marilyn Rider is sitting on a white slab, Treasurer.
Her triumph over a strange ugliness culminates in tragedy:
she dies of cancer at the age of 17, mother of one. And
then, really just the most popular person in the school,
Gini Wyant, whose older brother had been Class President,
whose sisters had been Secretaries and Treasurers,
she too is elected and photographed with a smile
slashed into her features. And here is the School Council,
a group of tiny people inside a photograph cropped
to resemble a blob; everyone is staring down:
I believe they are praying, or searching their laps
                    Waterloo Sunset
The Basketball Champs have suited up to shoot baskets.
Walter Lipke is blocking a shot. He once asked me if
my father were a bootlegger. "It's important, " he said.
The girls in blue and green gym suits have won
the Volleyball Championship. Once again I examine their legs.
Who's she? She's really cute, with a sweet, open smile.
Dismal assemblages of children engaged in Activities:
Red Cross, that collected so many nickels to furnish boxes
sent to foreign countries where bemused natives
gaped at their contents; Orchestra, strident fart-blasts
and sawing bows which, like Frankenstein, recreate the cries
of a tortured being; Band, with its no-nonsense march tunes,
plus Assistants in Homemaking–these girls are busy
baking, reading recipes, and opening the cabinet–
and Library, zealous demons engaged in research,
employing the Dewey Decimal System,
and Stagecraft, those tall, silent, capable boys
who operated the movie projectors, and Cafeteria,
a small group of poverty-stricken children
obliged to suffer the humiliation
of being forced to wash their classmates' dishes,

scrape the disgusting left-overs into a sack or hole:
these children are clearly spiritually deformed at this point.
Facing them, in a tactless stroke of layout, is Leader Corps,
young men and ladies superior in athletics and leadership
who supervise the younger children. There I am,
pretending to be an athlete. At least I had the sense
to avoid Glee Club, where crazed music teachers
led the way up stylized mountains of song
into even more majestic sonorities.
The Yearbook Staff, More Staff, and Committee seem relaxed
and genuine. One of them is Madelyn Grove, a tall and lovely
gray-eyed beauty who spoke so softly
no one ever heard a thing she said
and didn't care, she was so pretty. She jerked
me off in the lobby of the Hotel Hilton in Chicago
in a dream two weeks ago. And then,
beginning with Jayne Adair, pages of rows of faces
framed in squares. Jayne was pretty cute; her father
owned Adair Typewriter Co., where everything
was expensive. Larry Bennett, who studied calculus, rode
a motorcycle and, five years later, fell from a six-story building
after scaling its facade. I saw him three years after that
in an air-conditioned car with his father. I shouted, "Hey,
Larry!" He didn't hear me. I guess the air conditioning
was too loud. And John David Berry, who had played third
base for the Kendall Thunderbirds, where
I was shortstop. Incredible Dot Bottenhad,
whose vast forehead and wild eyes
express her astonishment at being six and a half feet tall, half-
witted, the No. 1 laughing-stock of the school.
Next to her is G. Craig Bolon, left-handed, awkward,
brilliant, but who never beat me at chess,
not once! He usually conceded
by throwing the chessboard against the ceiling.
John Christoffersen, enormously strong, who liked
to hit his friends in the groin, to "scraunch" them, and
Fred Clare, who studied calculus and whose father disliked me
because my father *was* a bootlegger. Mr. Clare
succumbed to a heart attack a few years back. Tom Cox,
so "oriental" as to be invisible, and attractive Howard Crain,

whose mother owned and operated Aloha Flower Shop,
Jo Crider, whom I kissed once, for some reason,
and Howard Cunningham, my best friend in grade school,
and Bill Cupps, my best friend in junior high,
Fred Daily who looks like Larry Rivers, Lyle
Davis who played right field for the Kendall Thunderbirds,
with his face of the hick, and Judy DeCamp,
oddly civilized and vaguely not unpopular, and
Tommy Dempsey. I pause here
for Tommy Dempsey. One foot tall, chubby, hair
cut by a lawnmower, teeth jagged, wheezing,
a voice like bedsprings, irascible, ornery, irritatingly happy,
the object of absolutely everyone's contempt,
I give him to you, world, Mr. Tommy Dempsey!
And Ted Duncan, who set the school on fire
lighting a cigarette in a wardrobe full of costumes;
Carolyn Duck, confident, comfortable, sexy,
but now that I remember her, not really very sexy.
Donnie Emerson, thin, dry, brittle, intelligent
and worse than contemptible; Michael Eoff,
pronounced "Oaf" but invariably "E-off" by gym coaches,
short, overweight a little, deeply embarrassed to undress
in gym and have his name disfigured day after day,
actually a bright boy whose shyness kept him away
from everyone. Diana Finn ("nniF")
whose boyish sociability made her popular with boys,
and Kay Finn, whom I never noticed until now: she's
very pretty. I must have mistaken her delicacy for weakness.
Jim Funkhauser, know as "Fuckhouse,"
and Warren Gandall, a smart-aleck
who once sneeringly told me he'd give me a quarter
for a "blow-job." I didn't know what a "blow-job" was.
Gandall had, it so happened, an enormous cock, but
I guess he figured it was worth only a quarter. Money
values have changed. Right near is Charles Godbold (sic)
who also had a giant cock. Further down
I locate Sam Graber, who
came to the school new in the ninth grade and whom
I befriended, only to have him steal my girl, the asshole!
Oh, lovely Madelyn Grove again. She has such lovely eyes.

Here with pudgy eyes is Charles Hargrove, whose father
taught at the local university. I told Hargrove
about Plato in the school lobby one morning, and
here's Hilary Henneke, whose father, coincidentally,
was heap-big President of the University.
Hilary had been to London, Paris, and Tyler, Texas, and
her sophistication (that is, her tolerance of our boorishness)
put her in a class by herself, so to speak.
Here's Phil Hull, who had a paper route
and legs like a grasshopper, and Gary Hart, whose father
embezzled funds and lived next door to my grandmother.
"It just killed Gary when his father went to jail," she said.
Roger Johns, one of the real studs, who passed out in Metal
Class because his best friend had hit him in the balls,
just horsing around, and Tom Lieser, a good friend
of mine who studied calculus, invented "leg spasms"
and was the most wacky person at Wilson.
Next to him is Viva Lillard,
who had been my girlfriend in the fifth grade
and with whom I had had a passionate and interesting romance.
She was a lovely girl and I'll bet she still is.
In fact I'd call her up if I knew her number.
Viva, if you're reading this, call me: area code 212,
local number 477-4472. Lynn McClaskey, whom I loved
madly and who kissed Sam Graber on New Year's Eve.
Here's Jimmy Meredith, who was getting handsome,
known simply as "Meredith," and Gary Meske, well
over six feet tall at age fourteen, who led our basketball team
to victory by getting 107 rebounds in every game,
and the great Leon Mooney, weighing in at well over 275
    pounds also at age fourteen, and who lived a block away and
    whom I actually liked! He ran the mile in a little over twenty
    minutes. The coach used to praise him, saying, "Look at
    Mooney here–he gives it all he's got!"
And Charles Mortin, a plumber's son
I believed to be very wicked, and who was, no doubt,
and Yvonne Mullen, whom I believed to be very wicked
and wasn't, I'm sure, and here is a cross-eyed girl
named Mary Helen Niemeyer;
John Orth, with the reserved manner of a Librarian, and,

wearing the expression of a person
who has just been informed
that he has won a million dollars
and the right to be immortal,
Ronnie Padgett,
wearing a red and white checked shirt and a crew cut,
followed by Anita Page, better looking here than she was,
and Jimmy Pommeroy, who was so modest, slow, and kindly
that everyone took him for the imbecile that he was.
I love this picture of Melanie Puryear:
red lipstick, real blonde hair, doo-wop,
a sultry Elvis Presley smile, and a sensational signature
flaming beside her face. She was one of the school Dream Boats,
　　who not three year earlier had claimed she loved me.
　　　　　　　These other faces, hundreds
of them, facing out, boys with hair like swirling ice cream
and girls so ordinary that I simply cannot believe it.
Ah, but here's David Shreve, as proper as Clifton Webb,
colorful Norma Tandy, who liked my eyebrows, Lee Tatum
whom I despised for no reason, and Linda Thomas,
the first girl who ever "gave" me an erection,
without knowing it, of course. We were dancing a fox trot
near the end of the ninth grade; her thigh....
And Jimmy VanBuren, whose father died in his sleep
of a heart attack, and Jimmy became
the head of the family, shed not a tear, moved
to Massachusetts; Howard West, who hid his chips
under the table when he played poker, who
joined the Air Force and rode through the air in a jet;
Jim Wise who fell in a hole; Lynn Yelton,
whom a few years later I would find attractive, too late, alas.
Twelve people entered school too late in the year
to have their pictures included. And then

　　Ronnie
　　You're a
　　real neat guy.
　It's really been nice
　knowing you these

3 years. Even though
    you are going to Central
I will still see you sometimes.
    Good luck at Central and
always. Your're a real brain boy.
Have fun at Central.
    Loads of Luck Always,
    Lynn McClaskey
    P. S. Have
    fun in Latin
    next year! Keep
    up your great
        smash!!!

Licked by Igor

As I lick the back of the head of a man named Igor Sikorsky and
then push his face down with my thumb and give it a thump with
the meat of my fist, I glance up to see Connie the postmistress ex-
tending her hand with my four cents change in it. Our eyes meet,
and for a moment neither of us is certain what to say. We are so used
to joking with one another, but something about this Igor Sikorsky
has made us sad.

Clunk Poem

I pick up the pieces
and stick them together.
They remain far apart,
so far apart I can't
even take them apart again,
so I add them to other
such clusters, and then
I have an idea: I will
go down and make myself
a peanut butter, blueberry,
and banana effigy of Hitler.
That'll show the bastards.

64

Stork

As I write I keep looking back
over my shoulder to the spot
where the road comes out of the trees
and stops in our yard, as if I'm
expecting a stork
with an actual baby suspended
in a diaper from its long beak,
the way they used to. When I had
a birds-and-the-bees man-to-man chat
with my son (age four or five) and told him
in the nicest, neatest, healthiest
way how babies are made, he thought
for a moment and said, "Nawww."
If a stork were to alight this very
moment where the shade cuts the light,
I'd look back and think, "Nawww."
I wish it'd happen.

Medieval Yawn

Who really sees anything when he yawns? The boy bent over his al-
gebra textbook is starting to yawn, and then two or three other
yawns blossom around the room. But none of the students has seen
the others, the contagion has been silent and invisible. Down in the
boiler room, old Mr. Harris has just plunked down in the tattered
easy chair next to the fuel line, but now a blank look surfaces in his
face as he remembers that he left his magazine in the tool room.
Maybe he doesn't really feel like reading today, anyway, though the
pictures would be nice to look at: in the distance a snow-topped
mountain, with dark forests somewhat lower, almost down to the
level plain, across which an army of medieval warriors is sweeping
toward you. They are coming to demand the return of young
Gretchen, the blond girl who got carried off by Sigismond, he
whose black hair flashes blue in the forest light. That's where his
head is now, in the forest, along with the rest of his body, which is
only partially clothed, alongside the body of Gretchen, whose body
is also partially clothed, and around which the light is exploding

silently, as the advancing army starts to dematerialize, as if erased,
like a problem with two unknowns that turns out not to be a prob-
lem at all simply because the bell has rung and everyone is moving
quickly toward the door on this Friday afternoon, 3:30.

Poem for El Lissitzky

–Bgawk!
There goes that Polly again!

The big storybook closed
and it was bedtime for real…
all little children go to bed now,
and sleep you well inside your pajamas,
and let your dreams rise softly
as the bubbles on the decal
over the headboard

by which you sleep
your wooden sleep,
little wooden children
with ragged edges
that must be sanded.
Time is the sandpaper–
isn't that original?

"Time is the sandpaper,"
I said as the housewife
opened her door to me.
I was selling vacuum cleaners door-to-door.
Once they let me in
I sweet-talked them into the bedroom,
where once again I said,
"Time is the sandpaper."
This time they swooned.
Never did sell many vacuum cleaners, though.

Chocolate Milk

Oh God! It's great!
to have someone fix you
chocolate milk
and to appreciate their doing it!
Even as they stir it
in the kitchen
your mouth is going crazy
for the chocolate milk!
The wonderful chocolate milk!

The Sandwich Man

The funny thing is that he's reading a paper
As if with his throat
With the bottom half folded neatly under his chin
Which is, incidentally, clean-shaven
As he strolls absently toward us, toting a sewing machine
On the front
With delicate little gold lines curling and swaying below a white
    spool in the afternoon
A dog barks—well, arf! you pull the cord attached to the monastery
Bell that rings utterly somewhere else
Perhaps the cord is ringing
And you are Russian
In some hideously small town
Or worst of all
You're listening to the story behind the bell
A history whose rugged but removed features
Resemble those of the sandwich man
Not the one that wandered off into the swamp
Cuffs filled with wind
And was never seen again
But this new one who overestimates his duty by teaching
School in a place that has as students
At best only a bunch of heavily panting dogs
Seated in rows of wooden and iron desks linked
Like slaves on a dismal galley, the Ship of Genius

Sailing for some points known and a few unknown
Caring little about either, huffing away
Toward the horizon destroyed by other students... *estudianti*

One of these others, the head, is in fact the Infanta,
In reality only a very intelligent little girl
But beyond the immense corrugated brook we know of as this earth
Covered with raving, a constellation in the shape of a bullet—
She always did love the sound of a ricochet—and I too
Can hear it often, at night, before I go to sleep
In my nose
            In Spain, ah
In Spain there are the prune fields and the dark
Beauty of a prune now lowers a shade
Past the sewing machine, over which blow long, regular waves of
    dust particles
In one of which a medium-sized boy in white sandals is peddling
    up to
Offer you a worried rose

Rose... but I know nothing of this rose
Although I will draw it for you in words if you wish
Clockwise beginning at noon on the outer rim
On the first petal is a cave and the second a squiggle
The third a proper noun or else a common noun beginning a
    sentence
Or perhaps a noun capitalized for no reason at all, for God's sake!

Japan! Penitentiary!
That's what we want!
To move and dance
With strangers, people we don't know
With lines and circles going though us
Who are the landscape

Whose clouds are really toots from the nearby factory
I love so much, the steam factory, making steam
For people to fall down on and permit their bodies to vibrate
Occasionally a straw hat is flung through the factory window
And sails spinning into the water

It is night

A dog barks outside the window
Either that or the window's silent in the dog
—You'll say I'm playing the overture
And finale off against each other, after all
There's no other way to locate the middle,
Which is more elusive than it might seem:
The fifty yard line does escape
The gridiron, extending itself through
Both grandstands, through you and me, plus
A parking lot now indistinguishable from the fog, backyards, dreams,
    washing...
And the large peanut that has come to stand for something beautiful
    and intelligent
In short, civilization.
"No so!" says a man in striped pants wheeled in out of the moonlight
"You think this only because you associate this object with yourselves
...which is okay by me...."
He was wheeled out and chucked over the balcony
Into the magnolia bushes.

At dawn, I find one other example, though nearly driven away
By the dust on it:
You are, say, six feet tall
Or six feet long,
In the first instance you are an active human being other than a baby
In the second you are either a very large baby or
A corpse or perhaps a bed-ridden invalid or
Two yardsticks placed end to end. What your six feet
Would be were you tilted at a 45° angle
I do not know
Doubtless a census taker's nightmare, in which bent
Horrible monsters jump out and bite him.

The next step is to know that this fuzzy angle is true in your heart
But not to know what happens to it
When it leaves there, flowers gushing out....
It appears in Amsterdam always
City of extension cords
And ladies with boxes of rubber bands and
A truly horrible music washing the streets rushing below the
    pigeons

That now seem to be following him as sure as iron
Follows a crook
I don't think I can stand it! the birds
Are swooping down in and out of a large design yes!
A police car is pulling itself together
In the skies, its headlights on now
Bearing down on the sandwich man, still reading,
Whose next step puts him behind
Us as we turn around to see his other board
And the horrible license plate on it

The Farmer's Head

At that instant there came a crash more terrific than any that had
preceded it, and the whole place glared with intense light. Everyone
was momentarily stunned, and when they recovered their senses,
Ernest, looking toward the farmhouse, saw a sheet of flame coming
from the farmer's head.

"Fire! Fire!" she shouted. "Your head is afire! It's been struck by
lightning!"

"By gum! So it has!" yelled the farmer. "It's blazing!"

He was rapidly shouting this as he ran from the barn.

Big Bluejay Composition

Compositions in harmony

the sunlight rods over the Commuter's Spa
                              bluejay

                                                                    oh

I don't want to go in
and watch Gene Tierney on TV moonlight

when   the shadow of a doubt

70

                    tiptoes down the hall

                                    crumpled tossed in wastebasket

Rainbow Colored Pencils made by Eberhard Faber
     maker of Mongols

ie Children of Paradise

                                    gray line wiggle

           a large permanent flinch

     just under the skin then

She turned to me   in the flying starlight

in the   in the

           tiny (there are no straight lines in a curve) breeze

breeze curving
           moonlight

                    when the m-moon shines
                    over the cow's shit

                                    bzzzzzzzzzz

                                    bzzzz

the square of the sum
     of two . flashing . numbers from the now on bzzz

suddenly the onions replaced the onusphere

     —to leon the counterpoint—   and Tommie Vardeman
     stuck his

head out the door a very old auto racer

gray wearing glasses

bluejay

sweet as stops

I catch my breath   I cry (cont. p. 42)

of planetary music

heard in trance

well the figurine of the bluejay

½ in the dimensional side of God

the earth is still–
…stars…stars…

God is in a trance,
now's the time to compose a few immortal lines

re's the immortal paper?

e immortal brain?   star

we go trot

trot-trot
past the abattoir

sliding 1968 sliding

————————————————

under the beauty of

broken thunder

he goes over center
k-boom   softness is northern

alert

alarming

the north,

le même nord où la mission Albert agonise maintenant
    parmi les cristaux

that is the wild blue yonder

screwed onto a bolt from the blue

magnetic,

the pursuit of Hedonism emerges boink from unwrinkled clouds

while… trumpets… Haloed, long pause

from across the ocean long pause

came gunshot

a piece of rain fell and hit the horizon

Slowly I turned…

behind us loomed the awesome figure of the gigantic
baked enamel ape, which Professor Morrison had, with
fanatical patience, constructed over the years.

                                        A bluejay

Tennessee raised in the dark

to the highest power

                        Tennessee is the *n* it made

I have spoken

            — — — —

                        I am speaking

like a sunset going down

                        behind

the rising dawn

            to ♪ot   mother,

Remember me   in your semi-conscious prayers   hit the
                                                brakes

when the dew is glistening on the bluejay

            and I go walkie to nightmare school

and the refinery is blasting away

Process and Reality   on this damp, foolish evening

bl

                                                    here

          the future
casts a pall bearer on the present–in the future the present
          will be

a thing of the past   losing altitude

          You shake

                    No

your head No

the smell of coffee on a morning the smell of hot coffee on a

          winter's morning

the table is set in the breakfast room frost on the windows
sunlight

          lock into which Mr. Morrison is inserting his key
floods the hardward store ∧ the black and white cereal box
     the porcelain

the fresh peaches the milk +

Now our mighty battleships will steam the bounding main

                    people jetting along
a symphony of tweets
                         the light of the Eternal Flame

                              clearly visible

from where you sit

in those great, golden heights   no doggie
                                            in the neighborhood

        all the doggies have gone off to war to be male nurses

the moonlight on the earthquake

                into which many doggies fell

    plunged fiery and screaming

                                        in their machines

        . . .

gravely   the Statue of Liberty
turned and faced the nation, finally!

a medium-sized flesh-colored male sexual organ extending

from its inner ear,

"The period in history termed Modern is now over," it said

                                –CLICK–

the bluejay fluttered on its shoulder

"Y-you'd b-b-better b-b-believe it!" it cried wildly

Ode to Clemmons Laurrell

Immortal Clemmons!

immortal in my mind
      though when anyone's mind turns into mine
   you may well wake up
               in the arms of an autumn night
     whose enormous blossoming is your entire body

Always so kind!
to me
(so first I make a student
of the thing as it is
then one as it isn't
   one idea on top of the other)

    Mortal and immortal Clemmons!

   you who in 1961 were working in a plastic boat factory

      I look back

              see stars
              out in the back yard
   mother mowing the lawn
     at midnight

    So great

   to look back
     at the way I used to look forward
to looking back
           Old Mexico!

   No shit!
my future me
    a mirror I would gaze into
   New Mexico
     to see ahead of me

the person I was becoming

                                    Mexico

        the person
    I am

    Such surprise
             morning is sending its dark blue
across the skies

And with the smell of exploding alcohol 33
    watching the centuries
    we catch strange and interesting figures
        passing along the edge
                of a land of sky-blue waters

                    Hose Nose
                    Chrome Dome
                    Mr. Absent Offenhauser
                    Skinny Jack Pinpoint
                    Hector L. Stormwindow

I hear a voice
in the darkness
    it is the voice of Hector L. Stormwindow
        wrapped in mystery   followed by seventeen zeroes
      like the top of a mountain
                    but very alluring
              the austerity of its expression sailing
                supreme blitz finagle

Hello Clemmons
    Listen

              This is The Punk

I say

if you would go
          to other
     than where you are
                    you have only to stand still
                                   permit

                    yourself to be carried away
       & should you wish
                to travel at a greater rate
                    you have to move through your ideas
in the manner of a pedestrian

Here comes a pedestrian now
                    your insane sister Arlene Brain
          totally with a mind
          her bathing suit shining
                         sprockets of moving pink
          Wow!
                                        and as I drew near
                                        they leaped
                                        over the side of
                                        a bright idea

               they had

So I lean back against the willows

               just to be free again

     just to embrace the fleeting image

          of a monumental and disasterous chord

          struck on a defective Omaha

          Sky & clouds tearing apart at sunset

and the tones fading on waves

of rising melody

in the flowing geography of the sky

(   )

the rainbow resumes
its formal presence

over the colonnade

and a tremendous midnight is suffused
into the lemonade

and like a light
we go out

in a Studebaker convertible
to where the divine firmament
babbled down to the divided highway
— — — — — — — — — — — —

the car automatically
begins to go
when the machine is turned on
and the land moves

in daydreams at night

in my biggest sexual fantasia
the mugwump sighs in the afternoon

IDEAS AS SENSATIONS

Everything in the world preceded by
I think…
I think… it is the dawn

                    of a new morning
         of which you have no memory
                   one with both
                 itself and nothing else

the way nothing and zero appear to be   to the non-existent eye
                              the same size
              as they go up and down
         in the shadow of

                                        jump!

              Wonder of Wonders

Red Bendix

A red Bendix
belts out its great aria
into the afternoon's great area
little birds fly through
and around in, they
are blue and it is summer,
you lie in a white crib
with the sun on your face: this
is not a photograph, it is
not a memory, it is
something that really happened,
and when you see it that way
it is happening again
inside your mind. Inside your mind
the outside of your mind
seems very pleasant, but
as you home in on the center
it gets dark and there is
something there, something
utterly horrible!

Alphonse Goes to the Pharmacy

"For the third time, Alphonse, no, I will not go to the pharmacy with you tonight. You must obtain your powders and elixirs on your own, just as you must affix your peruke to your head each day on your own. I will neither go to the pharmacy with you nor affix your peruke. Not now, not ever."

Alphonse the miniature chihuahua did not suffer rejection easily. His big dark eyes expressed the full measure of the despondency he felt as he pushed his head into the little sombrero and turned for one last look at his mistress, then wended his way out the door.

Snow

The light pink cone, the light green square, and
the light blue sphere, your baby eyes receiving their
dancing,

and lords and ladies weaving patterns in the manor house
among the teacups and the straight lines of perspective
the Renaissance had imposed on the old crooked world,
    The Book of the Courtier replacing
    The Nature of the Gods, which wobbles around
in its various dubious and weird knobby arguments, elegant
yes
but was Cicero always like this? Castiglione
creates the motion of his thesis through its rhythmic,
stately, measured pace, I think…
        because a heavy coat of dust
has just buttoned itself around my memory
and the chocolate milkshake I had that afternoon
is clearer and more certain than the words in the book.
I was embarrassed to be an undergraduate at Columbia.

I could feel, though, the bite in the fall air and yearn
in some semi-magnetic way for the all-wool sweaters
of several beautiful undergraduates–but for what?
That we would stare tenderly into our light coffee
as pastel dawn spread along foggy Morningside Heights!

But now I think I know something,
that the pale cream trapezoid
has a laughter of pale blue little sticks inside it,
that the very big snowman
who invented the alphabet
has not yet melted,
that in dreams begin responsibilities,
that I am stark raving sane.

Ode to Poland

It is embarrassingly true
that you don't begin to die
until you begin to live,
embarrassing because it is a truism
uttered by big fat idiots.
I am a thin person, myself,

seeing the golden sunlight
of sunset radiant against red bricks
that appear quite ordinary, too,
lifting me out of my shoes and into some real
or imaginary sense of the Eternal

as I turn into the New First Avenue Bakery
where the girl is saying, "At home
our manners have to be perfect, I
have to set the table just so,"
the light on the buildings set just so

and Intellect extending its puny arms
toward some greatness of cognition—
only to have the proverbial bully
of Mystery kick sand in its face.

Back home I pound on the table,
knocking a lamp into the air sideways.

Straight lines appear in the air
around the lamp as it falls.
These are they.

Three Animals

THE BUTTERFLY

The butterfly
flies up like pow
der to a woman's face
and drifts down
like a woman's face to pow
der

THE ELECTRIC EEL

The electric eel
slides through the water
forming different words as it goes
when it spells
"eel"
it lights up

THE GIRAFFE

The 2 f's
in giraffe
are like
2 giraffes
running through
the word giraffe

The 2 f's
run through giraffe
like 2 giraffes

Gentlemen Prefer Carrots

I nearly went to sleep standing on a corner today.
The light turned green
People charged down into the street, arms
with bags and boxes
while I stood there disappearing.
And after dinner, forehead resting

on the table, I saw some gentlemen
eating carrots in a dining car
with a landscape whizzing past outside,
really fast trees and hills, varied sights
and views, and those carrots disappearing
into the eaters' mouths. I raised
my eyes: music on the machine,
light; and fall coming on.

Voice

I have always laughed
when someone spoke of a young writer
"finding his voice." I took it
literally: had he lost his voice?
Had he thrown it and had it
not returned? Or perhaps they
were referring to his newspaper
The Village Voice? He's trying
to find his *Voice.*
             What isn't
funny is that so many young writers
seem to have found this notion
credible: they set off in search
of their voice, as if it were
a single thing, a treasure
difficult to find but worth
the effort. I never thought
such a thing existed. Until
recently. Now I know it does.
I hope I never find mine. I
wish to remain a phony the rest of my life.

Detach, Invading

Oh humming all and
Then a something from above came rooting
And tooting onto the sprayers

Profaning in the console morning
Of the pointing afternoon
Back to dawn by police word to sprinkle it
Over the lotions that ever change
On locks
Of German, room, and perforate
To sprinkle I say
On the grinding slot of rye
And the bandage that falls down
On the slots as they exude their gas
And the rabbit lingers that pushes it

To blot the lumber
Like a gradually hard mode
All bring and forehead in the starry grab
That pulverizes
And its slivers
Off bending down the thrown gulp
In funny threes
So the old fat flies toward the brain
And a dent on brilliance

The large pig at which the intense cones beat
Wishes O you and O me
O cough release! a rosy bar
Whose mist rarifies even the strokers
Where to go
Strapping, apricot

Dog

The New York streets look nude and stupid
With Ted and Edwin no longer here
To light them up with their particularity
Of loving them and with intelligence
In some large sense of the word:
New York's lost some of its rough charm
And there's just no getting around it
By pretending the rest of us can somehow make up for it
Or that future generations will. I hear

A dog barking in the street and it's drizzling
At 6 A.M. and there's nothing warm
Or lovable or necessary about it, it's just
Some dog barking in some street somewhere.
I hate that dog.

Cufflinks

I am brother to the frankfurter
Not brother literally of course
That would be silly
To propose myself as such
What I mean is metaphoric
I am brother to the frankfurter
I place the frankfurter on a plate
And it is gone and I am
One frankfurter larger

The frankfurter has fallen from heaven
Onto evil days
It rode serene in its clouds
It gave off light
It was universally admired
It was Adam and Eve combined
But a great chicken entered the factory
And shook its body in outrage
Bellowing, "Why am I excluded? Why? Why?"
And it rammed its head through the factory roof
And aimed its beady eye at the heavens–
"Goodness!" cried the clouds tearing apart
And since then there has been a great chicken in the way of all this
So that now I am brother to the chicken too
Via the frankfurter

In Frankfurt the Frankfurters rise
And commit their terror-stricken deeds
And return to their homes in the evening and bolt the door
Against the plastic chickens
That stagger through the night there
Pecking and acting irrational

(I don't seem to have a very well thought-out philosophy,
in fact I have never made a sustained effort
to systematize my various fleeting ideas on the Big Issues.
Not that any such systemization would have to be an ultimate one,
in fact the first premise would disallow any such finality;
to set my ideas in order would simply allow me to see
how they look placed side by side one after the other:
they would, like optical illusions, change
before my "very" eyes. My not having done this
perplexes me and then sends me into a bona fide gloom:
perhaps I am as frivolous and idiotic as I say I am
when I wish my listener to insist on the opposite, which,
thanks to social form or a desire to please,
he does, she does
the laundry and billows of soft foam float out the door
onto the sidewalk and into the street. I think
to myself, "That's the cleanest the street's been
since it was liquid itself." The optimism required
for such an outré observation goes hand in hand
with the most Protestant–if you will–sense of propriety
which I possess to the extreme, while, paradoxically,
scorning Duty as a mechanistic ethos foisted on us
by fingers that wield lingering wisps of smoke only.
Making the best of it, stoical but efficient,
that's me, and efficient might mean one thing today
and another tomorrow because it's emotional as well as anything else
and this is commendable, come to think of it,
though dangerously near to opportunistic.
But right now I don't know where to take this line of thinking
and I'm thinking you might be getting bored with this first person.
Let me switch to an earlier train of thought involving the
    unconscious.
Everybody shares the unconscious whereas everybody isn't me,
I am my own particular self sitting here more isolated than I
    thought humanly possible–writing this poem has
    isolated me.
As for the unconscious, I have an inexhaustible source of images
    there.
                                                        Donald
Duck flies through the trees under a sky of exploding dirigibles.

"My goodness," he squawks, "what a hostile environment!" Etc.
I can tune in so precisely to my own thoughts
that they are in perfect focus, no fuzz,
but I cannot for the life of me trace them
all the way back to their origin. So for me
they appear from what appears to be nowhere, a point
of origin that in effect does not exist.
I would like very much to be able to go
back through that point and into

nuts? Maybe I'd go nuts!
It's a challenge. One night walking home
from a poker game about five A.M.
I noticed a prostitute strolling along the other side
of the street. No one on the street but us. The sun
would rise in thirty minutes. She was
unbelievably attractive: sleek, slender, young, beautifully dressed
with a long wool skirt that buttoned up the front, and she was
chocolate. I found it hard to believe she was a whore
yet she was, unmistakably–a man in a car
pulled up to the curb and discussed some matters with her,
then drove away. I thought, "What if she approaches me?
How would I justify my refusal? No money? Tired?"
It was a challenge I couldn't meet. The heart
has so much courage and then some but no more.
I look into my heart from time to time. I am clever
but basically honest, actually a shy person
who's afraid of having his feelings hurt
or pride wounded, in other words a person
whose self-image, that of a minor, is essentially correct.
But I have a strongly developed sense of Beauty
and I am touched by Beauty when I sense it
though I feel I have never once been able to use an experience of
    Beauty
in my own attempts to create it: it's as if
I'm alone, no poetry or art ever existed, no
vast and dazzling vista of some foreign strand,
no uplifting experience communicated to me in any way,
as if the entire weight of the Cosmos
were on my fragile shoulders

and some powerful fingers were poised
above a grand piano for a final, devastating chord.
I see the fingernails, clear and clean and fine
and the cufflinks: on them written in script
the word "cufflink."

But you never can tell
what might happen.
Jean-Baptiste Marie Alouette François-Jones
might be born any minute
to Mr. and Mrs. Arturo-Torres Helen Kafka
who are riding across the night sky
on shafts of silver light. Their
spurs jangle and glint like spurs
in the immensity of space. Is space
immense? Or is it vast?
Here today to discuss the question
is Mrs. Arturo-Torres Helen Kafka.
Madame, uh
where is she? She was sitting here
in this chair
uh
who took
that chair?
You will be italicized
like the tops of mountains that slowly crumble and slide
along the sides of their immensity: you
are far below, not yet italicized, watching the spectacle
with an excellent pair of Zeiss field glasses
which you stole from the Spanish ambassador this morning.
Consequently he was unable to locate his breakfast.
I mean, you might think it peculiar,
as indeed it is, I'll grant you that,
but the ambassador likes to have his breakfast
served on a tray several thousand yards from the villa,
so he can track it down like a wild animal
and blow it to pieces.
So without the field glasses...
...meanwhile the broken rocks continued to fall
followed by night: you hear the great rocks
pounding out some symphony that would have sent

Bizet screaming up through the earth, for the darkness
is a metaphor for modern man's existential dilemma.
The first thing I think of in the morning is
"Good God, another day! Incredible!"
And I dive whistling a merry tune into my clothes
and burst onto the street with radiant smile
and an irrepressible air of joy and exultant optimism.
Passersby mumble into their English muffins,
"Doesn't he realize the rocks are falling?" They turn
away and step into massive piles of dog dood.
Now they are really pissed off. Some leap right
out of their shoes and run down the street in their stockings.
The shoes scrape themselves off and plod onward
toward work. The elevator is filled with empty shoes.
All over the busy metropolis
the shoes are trodding, trodding,
they are leaving the offices and stores,
the tiny pink ones in kindergartens
and the clodhoppers at construction sites,
the terrifying white numbers stream from the hospitals,
the scuffed pumps from the thrift shop, plate-glass windows
kicked out by shoes escaping from the shoe store, all
heading along waves of force
to where a rock the size of a... what? ball?
is lying on the ground. Next to it
stands Mrs. Arturo-Torres Helen Kafka
as the shoes walk in and pile up
like goofy teenagers at a campus pep rally
forty years ago, about the time Mrs. Kafka
would have been a College Jill herself. Now
she gestures to the throng and they fall silent.
What will happen?
I don't know.
From a great green rent
in the sky a bright yellow bolt
of lightning strikes the stone
and when the smoke is fanned away
the shoelaces have come untied,
a massive spaghetti-like confusion
surrounds the serenity of the stone.

The stone is immobile.
It does not move.
It does not change.
It is not Chinese.
It is not mysterious.
It is not pretty.
It is not a stone.

Mrs. Kafka is growing restive,
she pokes it with a small manual thunderbolt in her Mrs. Kafka hand,
the hand of the Statue of Liberty.
She turns her head to gaze
through the green and dark brown woods
where sunlight sets its shafts into the water
and rocks look happy with the water rolling
around and over their bald stationary heads.
Far along back up the stream
some trees dart into the darker woods
at the sound of an approaching human step.
You could not outrun a deer,
how do you expect to catch a tree?
Don't feel too bad, friend,
nature moves in mysterious and wonderful ways,
such as the boulder that crushed a stick last summer.
Or is that the right word, "stick"?
That is your code word.
                    (A crowd
of onlookers approached the befuddled teenager.
"Speak!" they commanded.
"My name is Rodney Harlem, I live at 2254 Willow Drive
here in Beverly Hills, I have a sister, sane
enough to pass a driving test, who calls herself
Beverly Hills, and when the morning sunlight hits
Beverly Hills and Beverly oh Beverly
kiss me darling as I melt into the fading sunset
all red and orange and like rivers of goodbye
saying hello to our departing greeting...."
Here the Club members grew restive. Benjamin Franklin
pounded on his knee and rose to speak.
It was as though all Philadelphia

were suddenly shrouded in silence.
Only the quill of the secretary
could be heard by a fly which had landed
on the head of Benjamin Franklin's daughter
who was the secretary. "Gentlemen,"
he began, and the members of the Philosophical Society
leaned forward and craned their necks,
"you resemble a flock of cranes
across the wall of the Stork Club
in New York," and the volleys and salvos
of laughter that rocked the old brick cradle
of American tradition could be heard
all the way to the face of Ralph Waldo
Beverly, a stagehand
who barely spoke because his mouth has been removed
by a special process I am not at liberty
to disclose: liberty
is subject to wild variations.
It takes "longer" to walk down a new and interesting street.
It takes three times longer
to walk down two new and interesting streets, etc.
But when we sit at home alone facing the same view as ever
we might easily find ourselves free-floating toward
what we have the courage to call eternity. At other times
we forget all about the whole thing and zip
presto it's gone. The variousness of time
gives it an elusiveness that exceeds the mercurial
shifting of, well, just about anything you want to name.
Even great mountains change their height. And
planets in their distant, lovely flight. And
future-removing dynamite.
The French quote Heraclitus as saying, "On
ne se baigne pas deux fois dans la même fleuve,"
which translated literally reads, "One
does not bathe twice in the same river."
In English I have heard, "One
does not step twice in the same stream."
Let us examine the troubling discrepancy
between the French and Anglo-American interpretations,
without reference, dammit, to the Greek.

The Frenchman bathes while the Anglo-American steps,
the former in a river, the latter in a stream.
One is so useful, a participant, the
other so aesthetic, like a daintily turned ankle
placed just so by a passing cloud.
That cloud! Hey, cloud! It's
the cloud
that poets of the English language love.
It floats gray and free above
and below an all-pervading blue,
bright and perfectly extended, and
your brain is understanding:
my two-hundred-mile-long dark-haired reclining flying lady,
it was you I imaged as a youth,
trodding o'er hill and dale, striding
straight through mountains into math homework.
And dusting the venetian blinds.
The simplest problem consisted
of whether to buy paper with two
holes or three. I thought
people who bought two-ring paper were mad.
It fitted less neatly into one's notebook,
and if one hole tore loose, the entire sheet would slip out
and dangle in a most disagreeable way,
in need of ring reinforcers.
Yes, I went through school
inside a cardboard box: graduation
was your own present you burst out of

into what seemed an absolute liberation: you in socks,
the kitchen floors of the world suddenly waxed
and placed before you end to end, extending past the moon,
icebox doors flung open to light your way through space.

As the years passed, you found yourself
stopping for a midnight snack: Dagwood
sandwich here, cold chicken leg there. Why is there
no meal so satisfying as the midnight snack?
How is it that you can recognize
the chicken leg at midnight?
Because after years of reading Classics

of the Humanities and Philosophy, each
volume at exactly seventy-two degrees under a light rain,
you find they form a chicken leg
that left some distant planet the day you were born.

And they're off.
Small green horse is taking the lead
with blue and red horses in second,
black third and orange off to a poor start
with white left at the gate.
Into the near turn it's still green
followed closely by bed and red
with black moving up fast on the outside,
orange in fifth. Coming into the backstretch
it's red moving up fast on the outside, it's red
and green neck and neck, it's Christmas
it's red and green along the tablecloth,
red and green, with blue third and black
moving up. They're going into the far
turn with red leading by a head and green
second, black is moving up along the outside,
followed by white nine lengths back
and orange fifteen. Into the home turn it's
red by a length, green and black followed by
a pack of wolfhounds–get those dogs off the track!
The picture freezes here
The camera draws back to reveal a man
beside the screen, hair cut short and a pointer
in his hand. "Nine out of ten dogs prefer
Doggy Dogfood. Tests show–" and here he tapped the screen
with his pointer–the screen fell to the
floor with an awful clatter. On it the track
was bent into unrecognizable shapes.
Picasso smiled and approached his canvas.
It is 1908. He will paint
a great picture.
He will paint several. He will paint
paint paint! Many bad pictures also.
But the public will hail him as a genius,
an artistic genius who walks around in his underwear

with dark eyes that say everything and nothing.
It would be embarrassing to ask him what he means
by that look of his. I would like
to ask him a few questions. "Mr. Picasso,
excuse me. I know your time is precious
but our studio audience is wondering:
What's with the 'Ruiz'? Are you really as solid as you appear?
Did you ever learn enough French
to have any idea of what people were saying around you?
And why did you ruin the horse race???"
Eyes back to the screen–it is sixty-five
years later–it has been magically restored
and is suddenly set in motion! It's red
by a length, green and black are closing,
with… hey! orange and white have streaked
ahead in a blur, with blue, a gray blur,
even now with black and green and now with red,
it's the entire field moving neck and neck,
across the bright explosion
forming a stymie.
The judges study the photograph and knit
their brows with first-class yarn: those foreheads
will come in handy when winter comes.
But one has come loose, a thread is dangling.
One of the other judges notices it. Unconsciously
he reaches up and tugs at it, slowly unraveling the forehead
until nothing is left but
a bright idea in a bright emptiness,
a photo finish.

Untitled

On the album cover of my ten-inch *Kindertotenlieder*
are two squares floating in a cloudy sky:
in the left-hand square is the face of Kathleen Ferrier,
that of Bruno Walter in the right. I feel sorrier
for her being dead than him, because she was a woman
and closer in age to a *kinder*. I almost never play
this record: it is too beautiful, and too sad.

Tom and Jerry Graduate from High School

It is an English countryside
though not in England.
Two Englishmen stroll in it,
small figures in the distance
and down among the willows.
It is a year
that existed
in the mind of the painter
who also existed.
My overalls are half on.
My hands reach toward the moon,
clutching a teddy bear in one arm
and a blanket in the other
—I have four arms—
and as I face the sky
the stars in its eyes shoot out
the stars in your eyes,
when most men your age
are driving nails through someone's forehead,
who are driving nails through someone's dog,
which in turn lets out a small chuckle and rolls over.
His pattern in the dust
forms a question mark
and the litter bearers run into the jungle screaming.
The savage rhythms of life
pound in my idea of Wallace Stevens.
And each day is a sentence
in the novel your life is writing,
the way cream and the coffee and the cup
come together at the same time,
fingers, fingers, oh fingers that snap
with little lines of sound emanating,
sticks mysterious in the air,
and a bird is flying, bluebird,
onto the fence for me and my girlfriend
to observe. We are scientists,
young people who build for a better "tomorrow."
We have straight eyebrows

which equal about one cement block.
Get enough of those blocks together
and you could build a house around your personality,
the glass Indian that roamed the prairie.

Once he did. Now, forget it.
Too many smoke signals blown into the sky!
The sky being of course
just an idea, but one powerful enough
to have things blown into it
and disappear.
We have been blown backward through the empty sky,
like ha and ah reversed,
it was symmetry,
it was postmodern figurine oink,
it was Manager Alvin
roaming the aisles of the darkened theater
where modern life had shown its last film,
The Maltese Falcon,
directed by John Huston
and starring Humphrey Bogart
and a tingling Mary Astor
and a great jiggling weirdo menace played by Sydney Greenstreet
with a svelte and intensely funny Peter Lorre.
What a film!
"I'm sending you over, sweetheart."
What an amazing thing to say to anyone.
That is what I'd like to say to modern life in general,
which is not always a sweetheart, either.
A little like Mary Astor, though:
one minute you hate her,
the next you have this overwhelming desire
to rip off her dress and wad it up
as you approach her,
a Maltese cloud.
Yes, it has transported you, this scene,
a little too much. It is heady
like heaven, or Heidi in heaven,
that little by little you slip up into,
an ordinary man

in shoes that glow
a bright yellow.
And an orange lightning tieclasp.

The Benefit of Doubt

When I was at the age when one's intellectual training seems to happen by itself, I became quite sure about the value of doubting one's own convictions, on the grounds that it prompted one to reevaluate opinions that might be outdated or stale. Years later I saw that doubt allows us to dispense with the *missigosh* of being right or wrong, conditions virtually useless in making art, which is what I like to do. I also like to look at things.

Outside the window at this moment, for instance, is a visual field of green and brown, flecked with yellow, all of it shifting and swaying, then wobbling, then suddenly stopping and stretching—wait, that's a deer. And it brings a message from the King. I am to come to the royal court, as swiftly as this deer can fly. Up on his back I leap, and we're off, over hill and dale, down village lanes, past men with thick spectacles and nightcaps that drag the ground behind them, the village street cleaners!

At last the castle looms in the distance, with golden beams radiating from it up into the sky, projecting a song that would have us believe that inside the castle walls there are thousands of people working and singing joyously. I come to you as summoned, O King, although you are not there, and never were.

Second Why

I have always found Mark Twain to be a rather depressing character, especially in movies about him, and I have always avoided his books like the plague, hated even the titles; but why? He's like me, with whom I have this love-hate relationship! The psychoanalyst rose from his desk and approached with his trim gray

beard. "Young man,"
he said gravely, "you have nothing
to fear. Float now, out the door,
on a river of electrical confidence,

and give off sparks, and be a sign,
and when you will have gone
they will say, 'Jesus! what a guy!'"
Some clouds left the sky

and its blue was purer. It
was a lovely deep baby buggy
into which the universe had plunged,
happy and innocent as a baby
going goo-goo and its mother's
lovely legs crisscrossing in the afternoon,
with the light through the trees
the way it used to be in 1948,
so primitive but beautiful in a stark
sort of presentation, pine
trees clustered at the Cozy Pines Motel
where the dim pink neon is restful
and the prices are reasonable,
sane, civilized, benevolent.

Disgruntled Man

I brush the hair located on the right side of my head,
I brush it beautifully,
thinking of you. Then
I notice that the hair on the left side
is standing slightly higher than on the right,
and my head appears to be lopsided.
I don't want it to look that way.
So I begin to brush down the left side,
grimly, with a sense of purpose
devoid of pleasure
that drips down the well wall
toward some deep, dark and cool pool
in which only peace is reflected.

Soon my head is in balance,
but it has become a head brushed for bad reasons
and I do not like the face I see.
A man disgruntled
with the way he brushed his hair.

After Lorca

Pink paper with blue lines
very nice

blue sky with big white clouds
very pretty

Face with big smile
very interesting

Why this smile?
Why are you smiling?

Blue paper with big white clouds
very nice

pink sky with blue lines
very pretty

Ladies and Gentlemen in Outer Space

Here is my philosophy:
Everything changes (the word "everything"
has just changed as the
word "change" has: it now
means "no change") so
quickly that it literally surpasses my belief,
charges right past it
like some of the giant
ideas in this area.
I had no beginning and I shall have
no end: the beam of light
stretches out before and behind
and I cook the vegetables
for a few minutes only,
the fewer the better. Butter
and serve. Here is my
philosophy: butter and serve.

Three Little Poems

I call you on
the 'phone &
we chat, but
the way tele
is missing from 'phone is the
way it makes me
feel, wishing
the rest of
you were here.

In literature and song
love is often expressed
in the imagery of
weather. For example,
"Now that we are one
Clouds won't hide our sun.
There'll be blue skies…
etc." Partly cloudy
and cool today, high
around fifty, mostly
cloudy tonight and tomorrow.

4:50 and dark
already? Everyone
wants to be
beautiful but
few are. 4:51
and darker.

To Francis Sauf Que

1.

You think of everything:
Modern silence, where I go back continually
To you, as does everyone, it seems…

2.

We are getting younger, perhaps

3.

I "hate you hate you

4.

The man walks under the house
In the Renaissance, the plum etc.

5.

More data, adversity is like walking
In the sun which is shining on you
In bed, where you are with her,

                                                "everything like that"

6.

Now I love you again because of these roosters

7.

Yours is topography to me in my dim head. I'm sorry, the virgins.

8.

This color, orange, tries to remind me of you,
Orange slice

9.

And you are

10.

Sometimes I leaped at the wrong time
Or right time, this made you who shall receive
This scarlet rose with some sort of greatness happy

11.

I thought so, so you changed your fasteners.
I think I hate you more than anyone else.

12.

If only you knew how to ignore me

13.

Then symbolism gets a model today,
But you didn't believe in that, its flaxen gray–
And neither does the porch
More than these worth taking notes on

14.

I didn't hear you when you all did it

15.

I will kill you

17.

To envisage your doom (it), and,
"Get with it, kid"

18.

To be plucked at exactly 2:10 in the morning

19.

They faded en masse onto the yearbook,
The shoelace through six years of catatonia,
Of Gérard Labrunie and this

20.

So whose shadow is this, yours or mine? and why
Are there two of us here instead?

Strawberries in Mexico

At 14th Street and First Avenue
Is a bank and in the bank the sexiest teller of all time
Next to her the greatest thing about today
Is today itself
Through which I go up
To buy books

They float by under a bluer sky
The girls uptown
Quiet, pampered
The sum of all that's terrible in women
And much of the best

And the old men go by holding small packages
In a trance
So rich even *they* can't believe it

I think it's a red, white, and blue letter day for them too
You see, Con Ed's smokestacks *are* beautiful
The way Queens is
And horses: from a pleasant distance
Or a fleet of turkeys
Stuffed in a spotless window
In two days they'll be sweating in ovens
Thinking, "How did I ever get in a fix like this?"

Light pouring over buildings far away

Up here when someone shouts "Hey!"
In the street you know they aren't going to kill you
They're yelling to a friend of theirs named Hey
John David Hey, perhaps
And the garbage goes out
In big white billowy plastic bags tied at the top
And even the people go out in them
Some are waiting now
At the bus stop (for a nonexistent bus)
And I thought it was garbage!
It's so pretty!

If you're classless or modern
You can have fun by
Walking into a high-class antique store
So the stately old snob at the desk will ask
In eternity
"You're going where?"
You get to answer, "Up."

I like these old pricks
If you have an extra hair in the breeze
Their eyes pop out
And then recede way back
As if to say, "That person is on... dope!"
They're very correct
But they're not in my shoes
In front of a Dubuffet a circus that shines through
A window in a bright all-yellow building
The window is my eye
And Frank O'Hara is the building
I'm thinking about him like mad today
(As anyone familiar with his poetry will tell)
And about the way Madison Avenue really
Does go to heaven
And then turns around and comes back, disappointed

Because up here you can look down at the Negro
Or pity him
And rent a cloud-colored Bentley and
Architecture's so wonderful!
Why don't I notice it more often?
And the young girls and boys but especially the young girls
Are drifting away from school
In blue and white wool
Wrapped in fur
Are they French? They're speaking French!
And they aren't looking for things to throw
Skirts sliding up the legs of girls who can't keep from grinning
Under beautiful soft brown American eyes
At the whole world
Which includes their plain Jane girlfriends

She even smiled at me!
I have about as much chance of fucking her as the girl at the bank
But I stride along, a terrifying god
Raunchy
A little one-day-old beard
And good grief I really did forget to brush my teeth this morning
They're turning red with embarrassment
Or is that blood
I've been drinking–I ordered a black coffee
Miss

And then a black policeman comes in
Unbuttoning his uniform at the warmish soda fountain
While I pull the fleece over my teeth
And stare innocently at the books I've bought
One a book with a drawing
By Apollinaire called "Les fraises au Mexique"
"Strawberries in Mexico"
But when I open the book to that page
It's just a very blue sky I'm looking at

The Ems Dispatch

Opening up a mud duck
The sin of the hearth had made him handsome
Don't ever give me what continues to be the tan arm of the hero
As identical, these sums and the chance to disappear
By including the chamois
Though that's a fine mess, I wist
Titles, etc.   2. Two Veins.   followed, pursued, sought after
But the curse now
Laid you down in the patient tent
Where there are men, there are no men
Just what I wanted (lie) perfect (lie)
I cared for the boy's drawing of the horse to get going
Then the lovely shin quest
Into the untracked signal gun, flowers, birthdays, sonnets
Put the hot, sweet breath of your breath against mine enemy

Come with me the nurse ferocity
Streets streets and less equal streets
The sails being torn to pieces in the upstairs part
But in a few moments
Without themes space or the invisible table message
Under the legs "far" into the night our hut
Its flaming gates
And the invitation to commit bibliography
The proffered hand
Guessed we're on to each other
The lice looked up in astonishment
Didn't explain the available cardboard murder
Going on into the mail covered with rust and the box
The great shoe prediction sigh clock
No doubt about it the neighbor thought it over
The extra put on its countenance and clicked on off

Let my dog sleep
On the altar of girlhood
But polish around it, observing the priority of the bump
The close call packed away and sniffing at the edge

Light As Air

1.

It's calm today. I sit outside, or inside by the window, and look out,
and for a moment I realize my left hand is holding up my head. I see
the light on everything, trees, hills, and clouds, and I do not see the
trees, hills, and clouds. I see the light, and it plays over my mind that
it is any day, not today, just day.

2.

The wind is making the trees swoosh and the volume goes up and
down. I have been sitting here for some time, at first looking out
at the grass and trees and sky, and then, turning more and more
into my mind and its noticing things, gradually looking at nothing
of what was before my eyes. A great cutting slash arced across the
last turn of the mental pathway I had wandered down and up, and
was approaching me from the left. I cocked my head to that left.

Slash, slash in the woods. My legs chilled. I will wait until I hear it once more, then I will get up and go inside.

Silence.

3.

In times of trouble and despondency I turn to sportswear. I have just added to my wardrobe three pairs of pastel-colored shorts and four light-gray T shirts and a yellow cotton pullover so elegant and off-hand it must have been designed in France. I put on my new clothes, lace up my new white shoes, and see people. They say, "You look nice. Are those shorts new?"

"Yes, they are," I answer.

Then I go back home and sit on the porch under the sky in my new shorts.

4.

I look at you sometimes when you're not aware of it. I look at you in those moments the way a stranger might so I can see you better than I usually do. And in fact you do always look fresh and new and similar to the person I think of as you. I love the way you look. And I feel happy just to be here looking at you, the way the dog sits at the feet of us, his great gods. I sit at the feet of the thing that is you. I look at your feet.

5.

I take off my clothes and am in the air, me flowing through it and it flowing around me. I look to the right. The first cottages of the little village, the first houses of the town, the first buildings of the city: bones, flesh, and clothing. Air around it all. Air I cannot breathe, because I am also a structure I am moving past, a tomb, a monument, a big nothing.

6.

He is a man of many vectors, that assemble and reassemble, the way music comes first from the air, then from a piece of wood grown in air. Then the air is in a museum in a country you are not permitted to enter at this time because your vectors are not in order. You must go home and reassemble your rods and cones: night is falling, the soft gray mist of his breath.

7.

I dreamed I had become a tall hamburger piloting a plane going down in a remote jungle waving up at me with inexpensive green cardboard natives ecstatic at the arrival, at last, of their messiah. A radiant hamburger bun top opened above me as I floated softly into their gyrating angular green midst.

8.

I come to a mental clearing where I can speak only from the heart. Free of the baggage of who I happen to be, and of all the porters who must carry the baggage, and the exorbitant taxi ride into a fuller version of the same small personality, I take, for what seems to be the first time in a long time, a breath that goes deeper than the bottom of the lungs, and in the pause that comes at the end of that breath there appears a little mirror, light fog on it clearing quickly.

9.

The palm of my hand is in Sunday, groggy, sabbatical. The rest of me is in Wednesday, up there and to the left, in the sky. I see you need a light, though you have nothing to smoke. You left your smoking utensils in Thursday. Let me recall my hand and fetch them for you. There, now you are creating puffs. But they do not dissipate. They form shadow copies of my hand that is moving toward your face.

10.

It dawns on me that I'm repeating myself. Another day and there I am, calm outside in the air with my hand returning along its vectors. In this mental clearing the photons are jumping all around the savages. Suddenly the witch doctor brings his face to mine and shouts, "Mgwabi! Mgwabi!" pointing to my photons. I reach up and take the light from his face and fold it with the fingers on my hands and it dawns on me that I'm repeating myself.

11.

At the end of the light I raise my voice from down there to up here and you are not here. I could shout until the words change colors and it would make no difference. Your vectors are heading out away from the voice of my hand and toward what it is pointing to, that bright cloud over there, the one with the burning edges, handsome and lighter than air at last.

12.

A cold streak runs through the sky now the color of wet cement that forms the body of the man whose brain is at a height of more miles than can be found on earth. This emotional absolute zero is like a spine conducting thick fog and thin rain through him, and when the sun's vectors approach his surface they turn and move parallel to it. Who is this big cement man? And how do I know whether or not he is the same one who came this morning and threw on the power that sent the electricity branching through my heart?

13.

It's dark today. I sit inside, my right hand touching my head. I look at the floor, the fabrics, the smoke from my mouth. It's as if there isn't any light, as if part of things being here is what light they have inseparable from themselves, not visible. The table doesn't stand for anything, although it remembers the tree. The table isn't immortal, though it hums a tune of going on forever. The table is in Friday, with me, both of us here in this dark miserable day, and I have the feeling I'm smiling, though I'm not.

Oswaldo's Song

Be glad that, as the world is in various forms of turmoil, you don't have to worry about anything, for a moment. You lean back in your chair and let your head fall back, and you notice a spot on the ceiling. What is it? It looks like a miniature South America. It wasn't there before. The tingling in your feet was there, but you didn't notice until you had stopped thinking about South America, how romantic it might have been under certain circumstances. It is 1948 and you are standing on the verandah of a large manor house perched on the side of a cliff above which the moon has parked, and off in the distance an old man is gently strumming a guitar and singing about the day he met his young bride in their village. She was seven, he was barely eight. They ran through the village until they got larger and larger, so large their shoes didn't fit, and when they went to their respective homes that night, they dreamed of some day coming to America, North America. "That's enough, Oswaldo," says a man standing in the shadows, and the singing stops. A light breeze rustles the banana palms.

ABOUT THE AUTHOR

RON PADGETT is the author of many books of poetry, including *Great Balls of Fire, Triangles in the Afternoon,* and *The Big Something.* Among his translations are *The Complete Poems of Blaise Cendrars* and Guillaume Apollinaire's *The Poet Assassinated and Other Stories.* His work has appeared in antholgies such as *Contemporary American Poetry, The Paris Review Anthology,* and *Postmodern American Poetry.* Padgett's awards and fellowships include a Fulbright, an NEA grant, a Translation Center Award, and a Guggenheim. He has collaborated with the artists Jim Dine, George Schneeman, Alex Katz, Trevor Winkfield, Joe Brainard, Bertrand Dorny, and others. He lives in New York.

NEW & SELECTED POEMS

was set in Adobe Garamond, a revival of the famous Garamond typefaces that were based on recastings of sixteenth-century designer Claude Garamond's original metal versions. The Adobe version was designed by Rob Slimbach of Adobe Systems.